Dear Maeve

Dear Maeve

POOLBEG

This edition published 2013
by Poolbeg Press Ltd.
123 Grange Hill, Baldoyle,
Dublin 13, Ireland
Email: poolbeg@poolbeg.com

A catalogue record for this book is available from the British Library.

ISBN 978-1-78199-985-1

Printed and bound by CPI Group (UK) Ltd, Croydon, CR0 4YY

www.poolbeg.com

For Gordon Snell and all my friends with love

Contents

Part III: On Kith, Kin and
        Close Encounters

Part IV: In The Public Domain

Introduction

Drama, someone is supposed to have said, is life with the dull bits cut out. There are those, however, and not just Sigmund Freud and Sherlock Holmes, who contest such a simplistic notion and creatively demonstrate that it is in the nooks and crannies, the holes and the corners of daily living that we can discover ourselves, find some clues to the riddle of human existence and so keep plodding on. Maeve Binchy's extraordinary talent lies in her ability to take the little tics and habits, the murmurs and queries of life and, with a neat creative twist, use them to confront us with our own absurdities. Her column is itself a veritable psychopathology of everyday life.

But do not be deceived. Behind the apparent ordinariness, the airy grace and the fluent style lies genuine wisdom. Important issues bearing on the successful navigation of life's stormy seas are considered, summarised and dispatched. How do you tell someone that they've tucked their dress into their knickers? Should you correct your wife when she says "commodium" instead of "condominium"? What should you do if you see your son-in-law nuzzling a woman not your daughter at a nearby lunch table? When the rest of a newspaper bulges with news about confrontations in the Balkans, disasters in East Africa and stand-offs in the Middle-East, when politicians assume that every citizen is gripped by talk of balanced budgets and constituency crises, Maeve takes a subtle glance at the practical problems that confront us all – when if ever to put an elderly relative in a nursing home, how to avoid a Christmas argument that lasts an entire New Year, just what to do for and say to a friend who is about to die. When she does turn her sceptical eye on politicians it is to hold up their posturings, policies and proposals to a similar scrutiny – how do they affect the lives of what those in high places call the ordinary people but Maeve calls her friends.

Despite her reference to unasked-for advice, she does not advise so much as ruminate out loud like a sagacious therapist leaving you to take it or leave it. The best friends, she reminds us, are those who let you tell your unhappy story over and over again until you have decided what you must do. Just listen and murmur and resist the enormous temptation and the inevitable request to advise. Absolutely dead right and so difficult to do. The curse of today's living is not that there is nobody around to give advice but too many giving it too readily. She is not one of those urbane, emollient writers who manages to manoeuvre their way through a weekly column without offending a soul. She makes it perfectly plain she cannot stand unpunctuality, stoutly defends Dubliners' rights to be Dubliners in Dublin, even if that means preferring friends and neighbours to let you know before they drop in for a casual chat, and, in her now famous assault on Aer Rianta's decision to remove the buggy on Pier A in Dublin Airport, she provides a vivid demonstration of how unasked-for advice can pack more punch than a plethora of carefully implemented opinion surveys. Aer Rianta promptly restored Binchy's buggy and its daily peregrinations are a testimony to the power, passion and the persuasiveness of her prose!

Professor Anthony Clare

Foreword

A very elegant French woman I know once said to a total stranger in a café that he'd look much better if he wore his shirt loose over his trousers instead of belting himself in. I put the menu over my head in fright and thought we were both going to be thrown out, but the man accepted the advice for what it was, and we later saw him looking at his reflection approvingly in the window.

A journalist in London told me once that she was sitting minding her own business on a train reading a book and just twiddling with her hair. A man opposite her, who was just about to get out of the train, said "I hope you don't mind, but that is such an infuriating habit, twisting your hair around your finger, that someone may well murder you for it one day." Then he scuttled out, back to his suburban life. She checked with other people, and indeed he was right. It was the most maddening thing, it made her look as if she was auditioning for *Little Miss Muffet*. He may well have saved her life.

I didn't like the letter from Anon in Mayo who said that he or she quite liked me but why was I constantly picking my nose on television? I looked at the repeat of the offending programme and it was sort of a nervous tic. I kept rubbing my face, and it did look awful. So I don't want to get down on my knees and thank old Anon in Mayo, but at least Anon was more involved than anyone else.

And it was more or less thanks to Anon that the Unasked-For Advice column in *The Irish Times* came about, from which this book is distilled. One thing, Anon, does not lead to the other.

Clear-sighted, far-minded and practical, I could solve other people's problems at a stroke. What to do about my own emotional catastrophes, real or imagined hurts, maelstroms of indecision and confusion, of course, I have absolutely no idea . . .

Part I

Manners, Mores and Get Real Etiquette

WORKERS AT PLAY

"It is true, true freedom to know that you are not and will never be the centre of all attention."

Last year the office party was terrible. People became very bad-tempered. Her best friend got red in the face and shouted at the boss: "Why is it that we do all the work and you get all the money?" The boss replied mildly that this was the capitalist system and somehow, very unfairly, it was agreed that he won the round. The year before, this woman had entered into a short-term alliance with a colleague – so short-term that it was over before she had thought it had begun. But still there was the lingering shame, the embarrassment on her part, the quite uncalled-for smirk and belief that he was Jack the Lad on his part, and the vague office rumour that she was a bit of a goer after three glasses of wine.

And now it's party-time again. The restaurant has been booked for next Wednesday, the mini-bus has been hired, the expectations are growing, and she would give anything to get out of it. But nowadays she is more senior in the firm, and it would look bad if she didn't turn up. As if she were trying to distance herself, make herself important even.

She says she has played it totally wrong: she should have shown great enthusiasm for it, and then suddenly and unexpectedly got a diplomatic 24-hour flu. No one could have said she was lacking in spirit. But she has already let it leak out that she isn't looking forward to it; she has managed to ensure for herself the worst of all possible worlds. She has to go and they know she's going under pressure. If she does take a drink, she could well head, like an unguided missile, for Jack the Lad again; if she doesn't, she'll be called an old prune and a killjoy. Oh, she says, isn't it well for you, Maeve, working at home, no office party.

My eyes always narrow dangerously when I hear anyone saying isn't it well for anyone else. An awful lot of the time I believe that we make it well for ourselves or we make it a pain in the neck. Many a home worker will confide to another that we miss the office parties, we get cabin fever, we yearn for the office, any office. I have even invented an office party for the two of us where we wear paper hats at the word processor all morning, have a drink the moment we hear the Angelus and then fall into the Sorrento Lounge for our office lunch.

But enough about the increasingly eccentric and unasked-for details of my own private life, and back to the woman who has to go to the office party on Wednesday. Firstly, she should book a hair appointment in some place that stays open late . . . that will keep her out of the pubs for the warm-up drinks. No one could fault her for that . . . They'd have to say that God help her at her age, over 35 and everything, it's nice to see that at last she's trying, uphill struggle and doomed to failure though it may be. So that means she will arrive looking groomed, old but groomed.

At the hairdresser's, she should eat two sandwiches. To hell with years of being careful and avoiding carbohydrate. Great big sandwiches filled with things that will raise her blood sugar, like peanut butter and raisins and walnuts. Things that will give her instant energy but won't cloud her brain. The lovely thick slices of bread will sit like sponges, or wodges of oasis, waiting to soak up the drink which she should accept and even buy with huge alacrity and enthusiasm.

She should smile knowingly at Jack the Lad, ask about his wife and babies, and keep a half-pitying smile on her face as if she felt the wife had not done well in the brantub of life. She should be interested in everyone else's lives and loves and draw them out and find out their woes and their office rivalries. She should wear an inexpensive dress in a dark colour which will not suffer unduly if someone knocks a plate of untouched spaghetti carbonara over her, or pours the dregs of the last bottle of Bulgarian over her knees rather than into her glass.

She should know that, whether she is old or young, beautiful or like the back of a 46A bus, married or single, nobody at that office party next Wednesday is going to give her more than a moment's thought. They are all obsessed with themselves. It is true, true freedom to know that you are not and will never be the centre of all attention.

It is an amazing arrogance to believe that somehow you are the guest of honour at every happening, and that there is an interest and anticipation in what you will do or say, how you will look and where you end up at the end of the evening. Most people are far too interested in all these aspects of themselves to have more than the merest and most passing concern about anyone else.

Unless she hits on Jack the Lad again in a spectacular way, or gets into a dramatic debate on the nature of the capitalist system with the Chief Executive. she will not be considered worthy of comment. She should bring a lot of tissues in a briefcase. In case other people are weepy or sick.

She should have sticking plasters (people are always

cutting themselves at office parties) and painkillers (you can see the headaches forming over heads like ectoplasm). She should bring safety pins – clothes always come apart on these occasions. She should tell herself 11 times that she will contribute no office gossip whatsoever. Amazingly, even the most howling drunk will have a moment of clarity for the one indiscretion that you most regret having let loose. I know this may make her into a cute hoor but the alternatives are being a self-centred diva or a party pooper. She should drink a glass of water for every glass of wine, she should not order anything that has to be flamed either at the table or on its way there – flaming dishes and office parties don't mix.

She should say that she'll stick with the wine instead of port. No matter what anyone says about it being good with cheese, it's the thing that crosses your eyes in your head. If anybody asks whether she would like a slammer, she should say no thank you. She doesn't want to know about slammers. If they ask her to sing, she should say she will if someone helps her with the words, and she should begin with "I would do anything for love" because that's all anyone knows of it anyway and they'll all join in and roar it out and think she was a good sport and wasn't it amazing for a geriatric in her thirties to know that this was the right song to sing.

And then on Thursday she might send me a postcard agreeing that nobody there took a blind bit of notice of her any more than they had done any other year. That it was all in her mind, and thanks to my good advice about the sandwiches and everything else, it wasn't still churning around in her head and her stomach.

CANCEL THE SHOW

"I advise them to remember the marvellous song that Noel Coward once wrote asking 'Why Must the Show Go On?'"

They have had a lot of things to spend money on and business has not been good. The recession. But is it?

Other people seemed to have survived the recession. They have new cars; they have Christmas plans that would make your head swim – a Sunday lunch party for 30 people; 10 kids going to the pantomime; New Year's Eve, staying overnight in a hotel, 30 miles from Dublin.

That doesn't sound like recession. They have had a red alert on telephone and gas bills. And now it's coming up to Christmas. They have to take part, they say, otherwise leave the human race. What explanation could they give that wouldn't sound like being as mean as hell or moaning when others are able to put a face on it? Everything costs so much, but nobody else they know of or hear of or read about is drawing in horns, so what does that make them if they take this stand?

They look at the shop windows – everything is so lush and extravagant. They read the suggestions for gift giving that seem to involve presents that would cost £15 to £20 a head, for people who are not immediate family. The toys and games and gadgets advertised on television, and everywhere, for children are even more pricy. Would it be ludicrous to put a notice in the paper saying you weren't giving presents or sending cards? Well, yes of course, papers love advertisements; it's what pays our salaries in fact.

No, it wouldn't be ludicrous. A lot of people do it for the

best of motives. But is it necessary?

I don't think so. I think this angst-ridden and impoverished couple are making themselves over-important by going to such extremes. There's no law saying they have to give people expensive presents or send them cards. There is, of course, the tradition and the feeling of guilt about not reciprocating someone's generosity.

Still, there are ways of lessening their guilt considerably and also of heading other people's generosity off at the pass.

Take cards for one thing. They used to send about 90 to 95, probably 100 this year, if the truth be told. Well they needn't send any. That would save them 100 times 28 pence and, suppose the cards cost 30 pence, there is now a total saving of £58 in hand. But they'll look so *mean*, so shabby, so forgetful, uncaring.

I wonder. I really wonder. There may be about 10 they should send, to those who get few Christmas greetings and might be counting on them. But who else is going to be wandering around their over-garlanded house, pacing the floor, waiting for a Christmas card from this couple to drop onto the mat? Do they really believe that they are going to be worthy of gossip or even the passing hostile thought from anyone to whom they do not send a card?

That way madness lies. I advise them to say nothing whatsoever about the drastic curtailing or even near abandoning of their Christmas card list. To draw attention to it is only to invite minor resentment. Exchanging Christmas cards is not an international treaty or a business deal, it's meant to be a goodwill gesture, a kind of wish. If anyone is barking enough to feel slighted by the lack of a Christmas card, they don't deserve one ever again.

Now on to presents which are a bit different. Years ago,

when I was on worse than red alert about the phones and had actually reached red cut-off, I couldn't give Christmas presents either. So I didn't pretend. Nor did I give anyone a huge and pitiful explanation, because I was afraid it might look like self-pity or worse still, a plea for some kind of a hand-out.

Instead I went out and got everyone I should have been giving a present to a great clump of holly. I went to a friend's house down in the country with a big secateurs and I chopped and chopped, then he gave me six sacks and put me back on the train to Dublin, the most dangerous passenger they ever had.

I tied them up in individual bunches and gave them to people with the slightest and most minuscule explanation about wolves being very vocal at doors and hoped they might find these early Christmas decorations nice, instead of a Christmas present. I said the words "instead of" fairly heavily so that you'd have had to be brain damaged not to know that this was your lot.

But nobody ever gave me a food parcel or a pat on the hand or a lecture on the virtue of poverty. As far as I remember, they all professed themselves to be delighted with these dangerous bunches of holly. They said it was highly imaginative and maybe they gave me something a bit less than lavish that year, which was the way I wanted it.

But the great thing is that I know in my heart that none of them gave two damns about it one way or the other and that, when times got better, presents would look up and, if times had not got better, it wouldn't be the end of friendship.

What might well be the end of friendship would be an inane getting-into-debt to give someone four cut-glass, brandy tumblers that they couldn't put in the dish-washer, which would set the pair of them back the entire Christmas grocery bill. And that would only be one gift to cross off the list. I advise them to remember the marvellous song that Noel Coward once wrote asking the question "Why Must the Show Go On?" If the show is going to drain them, bleed them dry and worry them to death, it's no show worth having.

At a time that has always been meant to be one of peace and goodwill, they should realise that most people are normal and that their friends are bound to be normal and not human calculators, counting the gifts in and counting them out. If they have anything to spend, let them spend it on their children or on other people's children.

They probably know all this already but in a welter of Christmas over-excitement, with the place coming down with advertisements for luxury gifts, I urge them to remember it. Friends who cease to be friends because they don't get a pop-up toaster, or something with a plug on it, *deserve* to be discarded in early December.

OFF TARGET

"We tell people if they have spinach on their teeth, why not tell a woman if she has lipstick in her moustache?"

There's this woman who used to be a real smasher some years ago. Although she was used to being admired, she wasn't a peacock or anything. About ten years ago, when she was in her late 60s, we had lunch in a smartish place and she asked the waiter if he would go out and get her an evening paper because she wanted to look something up. And the waiter quite courteously said no he couldn't. She sighed and without any affectation said to me, "I forget I'm not beautiful any more."

It was as natural as saying you weren't a teacher any more, or didn't have an account in such-and-such a bank any longer. She had been so accustomed to smiling and dazzling people into doing things for her by sheer good looks. I said that she was still beautiful and she asked me a favour. If ever she started to look ridiculous, would I tell her?

She wasn't choosing the most sensitive and discerning of people to advise her in this regard, and I told her this. My idea of ridiculous might not be spot-on. But anyway, I said I'd do it if I noticed, and she seemed pleased.

Now she is in her late 70s, her marbles are in great order but her sight is very poor. She is throwing make-up at her face, and mainly missing. There's a big red gash in the area of her mouth and she puts that very bright blue eyeshadow on with a heavy finger. And as a result she looks terrible.

People speak of her sadly. She used to be so lovely, they say, and isn't it tragic to see her trying to make herself up as if she were still young and attractive?

I don't think this is what she is doing. It's not a question of disguising mutton as lamb or anything. It's just that she can't see it. I can't *bear* for her to think that she looks great because she has put on the war paint and for it to have misfired as badly as it has.

If you saw someone with their dress tucked in their knickers, you would tell them, wouldn't you? It's not the way people are expected to emerge from the Ladies. And the sooner you tell them the better, there will have been less of an audience for the spectacle.

So in theory it's simple. You tell her. And say that you think the hand that applied the foundation may have been a bit heavy and the light in these places is monstrous, they should be prosecuted for not having kinder shadows for us to lurk in. And you change the subject sharpish.

But wait a minute. Her face was what people knew her for. She might think it still more or less is. You might destroy her self-confidence, and the gutsy spirit that allows her to lather on all this stuff. I remember well some thundering bitch saying to me, "Oh I *am* sorry. Did we come to collect you before you got ready?" And I *was* ready. This was as good as it got. It's seven years ago and I remember it still.

And does it matter that she looks like *Whatever Happened to Baby Jane*? Amn't I the one who's always saying that only fools judge people by appearances? And remember the tiresome neighbour in London who says "I speak as I find" and, unfortunately, she almost always finds something unpleasant?

Is there an argument for forgetting to be the arbiter of elegance and ignoring it? After all, I am somewhat cosmetically challenged myself in terms of blusher and lip-gloss. Have I the right at all to mention anyone else's attempts?

And is it taking a chance remark, made a decade ago, a trifle too seriously if I say that I promised I would tell her? This wasn't some oath – marked by the exchange of blood. Almost certainly she has forgotten the request and my pompous delivery of the promised advice might come as a very unwelcome bit of news.

You could talk yourself out of it with ease. Why invite hassle, why criticise and upset? Why disturb, gratuitously, another person's equilibrium?

But. And it's a big but. It's not telling her that she is old and trying to alter the natural progress of time. It's trying to cope with the fact that she can't see the dog's dinner she has made of the face that was so important. If she were 18 and had partial blindness nobody would hesitate about telling her that her hand had slipped. We would see it as a normal courtesy, as you would raise your voice for someone deaf, or move a chair out of the way of someone with a white stick.

This woman, who could literally make people turn around and look at her, should not be allowed to have a moustache unless she knows she has one and has decided – to hell with it. She doesn't have sisters and she doesn't have daughters. The normal chain of over-honest response is not there.

With less lipstick and a little grey eyeshadow she would look lovely. The bones of her beautiful serene face would be a pleasure to look at. She is not trying to pretend that she is approaching 50 rather than 80, she is dressing up in the way she dressed in her 40s and 50s, and without being able to see that it isn't working.

I got tired of people telling her how marvellous she looked, and then saying afterwards how sad it was to see her looking so gaudy and lurid. She may have many good years ahead, why must she try to read the sounds and try to interpret them without the information she needs? We tell people if they have spinach on their teeth, why not tell a woman she has lipstick in her moustache? I advise myself to tell her. Without apology, without reminding her that she *did* once ask me to keep her informed of any alterations.

She will not read this so it's not a question of doing it by stealth. I don't think it would be better to give her a voucher for a marvellous friend I have who runs a beauty salon. That's being even *more* patronising. I advise myself to tell her quickly and casually because what is being told is in fact not at all important. But what is important is the motivation and reaction of those who wish to give dignity and fear giving offence.

FIGHTING SHY

"If they have opted to stay in the human race, they can damn well greet people and be greeted without making some kind of virtue of Not Being Good In Social Surroundings"

Shy people say they don't understand extroverts. The people who define themselves as being shy say that it's all right for the rest of us. This makes me very cross. It's never all right for anyone. People have to *make* it all right. Those who smile apologetically and say that they are rather antisocial deserve a cuff in the ear, not sympathy. If they are antisocial, then why aren't they sitting out in a desert somewhere, eating low calorie locusts and honey and doing the hermit number in style? If they have opted to stay in the human race, they can damn well greet people and be greeted without making some kind of virtue Of Not Being Good In Social Surroundings.

Right. Now we know where we all stand.

So anyway, I got this letter from a woman who was going to a book launch. She had never been to one before, but the author had rented a flat from her while he was writing the book, and he had included her in the invitation list. She was both thrilled and terrified by the invitation. It crossed her mind to write to me.

Her friend said I was the *last* person she should write to because I hated etiquette books and would probably tell her

18

to act naturally. But, she said, she didn't know what was "naturally" for this occasion, so could I be a bit specific?

I gave this a lot of thought, mainly because I wanted to prove her Doubting Thomas of a friend wrong, and also because she's right. It's useless to tell people to "be themselves". It just doesn't work. When you're at a loss in a place, you forget who you are.

Or else there are too many versions of yourself that come to mind and you wonder which persona to bring to the fore. I felt she didn't want the *Practical Freeloader's Guide to Book Launches*, the kind that gives hints about going early, making friends with whoever is pouring the red wine, asking the waiter to leave the plate of canapés just there on the table beside you and avoiding eyes when it comes to the time to buy the book. No, she wanted to fit in and enjoy herself. And her main problem was that she felt, probably accurately, that she wouldn't know anyone there.

She was dreading a sea of roaring, chattering folk, all baying at each other, while she stood on the outside looking conspicuous, because she was a stranger. So 1 gave her great advice altogether. I told her to identify herself to everyone she met. It's one of the most important rules I have ever learned . . . and, if you do it without sounding like a fog-horn, it's a very attractive trait.

Now the so-called Shy Brigade, for whom I have so little time, tell you that it's arrogant to give your name before you are asked for it, but I don't agree. I think they are too selfish and self-centred to help anyone else start a conversation or be at ease. Whom would I prefer to meet at a book launch?

Given the choice of two kinds of people . . . would I like to meet one of the self-styled shy people, silent, uncommunicative, always with a little smile playing about their lips? All right, I know it's a nervous smile, but the rest of us are nervous too and we don't give off vibes of superiority.

No, I have had too many years of trying to put the shy at ease and got nothing but scorn for my pains. I have often turned into my Gestapo mode, trying to get ordinary, everyday information out of those who refuse to part with it. I'm giving up on the shy. Their self-consciousness is, in fact, a monstrous selfishness. I'm going to leave them and look for the people whose insides may also be churning but who can identify themselves, in the interest of the common good.

I would so much prefer this woman if she came to his party determined to help other people to enjoy themselves by giving them a basic and harmless opening sentence. She doesn't have to do it to the whole room. Maybe three or four times at most. Maybe only once.

A nice person who smiled and said "Hello, I'm so-and-so, I was his landlady when he was writing the book. Isn't this a great occasion?" I'd be *delighted* to meet her. Wouldn't anyone? She can give you loads of information. If you want to ask if he was starving in a garret, or if it was a penthouse, you can. If you want to ask if he had loud music or a colourful social life, it's all open to you. If you don't want to talk to her much longer, you can introduce her to someone else because she has given you her name.

I wouldn't think she was arrogant. I would think she was making an effort, and I'd applaud her for it. The guy who wrote the book has a million things to worry about . . . like, will anyone turn up? Will too many people turn up? Will the drink hold out? Will anyone write anything in the papers?

Will they write the wrong thing? Will the book die without trace or will it be vilified as the worst thing ever written?

What he does *not* need is the sight of his former landlady standing on the edge, twisting her hands and being antisocial and all those other awful things that shy people marshal as dignifying characteristics. He would much rather see her chatting away to people from other parts of his life. He will relax his shoulders momentarily and think that it was a good thing to invite her, and maybe, in a rush of gratitude, he'll give her a free book.

And this great advice about identifying yourself holds good in every situation. In places where people mumble introductions, or don't give them, always say who you are and say it with a slightly upward intonation, as if you are eyeballing them to repeat who they are too.

That way you might actually get to know who you're talking to and there can be no occasion when it's the wrong approach. Suppose whoever you're talking to knows nobody – then he or she will be thrilled with this piece of information. If the person knows everybody, the chances are that the brain cells are beginning to die off and memory overload is setting in, so he or she will be delighted that you gave your name, while protesting that it hadn't been forgotten.

Identifying yourself is the answer to any problems of shyness and awkwardness. I'm delighted that I was able to work it out so satisfactorily.

Surprise! Surprise!

"He died, the poor guy, because he thought he was coming home after a long, tiring day and . . . 100 red-faced, shouting people in party hats jumped out at him"

There is a surprise party coming up. It's a sort of anniversary or birthday or homecoming or graduation she said vaguely, determined not to give the fun away. If fun it is. Everyone is sworn to secrecy and we all have to be in place and keep quiet while an unsuspecting person or persons are led in to what they think is something else. Then the lights will go on and we will all shout and scream *Surprise! Surprise!*

The success or failure of the thing will depend entirely on the range of facial expressions we will witness, from shock/horror, to lumps in the throat, to tears not far from the surface, to hands clasped in amazement, to smiles and beams of delight, to head-wagging saying this was a terrible trick to play.

Maybe some people are great actors, and they can turn this kind of performance on to order. Maybe a lot of people are so damn nice and uncomplicated that these actually are the emotions they feel.

Perhaps there are people who *think* they are not surprise party people but rapidly become those very creatures when a friend puts them through it. It is even possible to argue that a surprise party can take the onus off someone having to plan a thing all alone, with all the worry, indecision and expense involved. But I only say all these things to show that my mind is not closed when I say that I cannot bear surprise parties and I think they are a waste of time and kindness and goodness and energy and that it would be much nicer to tell the person that YOU are throwing some kind of gathering for them and then make it as lavish and cast the net as wide as you like.

My American friend who runs 20 blocks in her trainers to work every morning and does, I admit, have an extreme lifestyle told me that she was at a surprise party where the honoured guest had a heart attack and died in front of them all. The organisers are still in counselling over it and people are still sending them letters of sympathy. He would have died at that moment anyway, the sympathisers say, his time was up. Like heck it was. He died, the poor guy, because he had thought he was coming home after a long, tiring day and too much to eat and he was going to put his feet up and watch a movie. Instead, 100 red-faced, shouting people in party hats jumped out at him. *That* is why he died.

I didn't know this man and it would be silly for me to get into some kind of retrospective outrage on his behalf. But I do know a woman whose husband had told her, on the eve of their 30th wedding anniversary, that he was about to leave her for a younger, shinier model. She tried to talk about it with her family and friends the next day but none of them would speak to her because they were so busy planning and disguising the limpest and dampest squib of a party that was ever held. Of course they couldn't have known, and naturally they had meant well. But can you think of a more humiliating, hurtful way to get on to the next stage in your life?

I know different people like different things. By this stage I may not know much, but I do know that. I had a friend who thought her boyfriend had forgotten her birthday and she had become very sad by the end of the day. He had actually arranged a great party for her in a restaurant that evening. At about 9 p.m., he pretended to remember it, and suggested they try and get a booking, by which time she had become quite tearful. Normally careful about her appearance, she wasn't in the mood to dress up so she just pulled on her raincoat. Of course she arrived at the restaurant to find 30 people dressed in fine feathers. She hates the photos of the night because she looks like Cinderella before the arrival of the fairy godmother.

And I also know a man who said he didn't want any fuss made of his 50th birthday and we all thought that's what he wanted but he was sitting eagerly all day apparently waiting for all the razzmatazz to start. And it didn't. Even his family had believed he didn't want to mark passing the half century and they had all glossed over it. And he had been getting ready for the one that never happened.

It's not that I don't love celebration, I celebrate things like "It's Wednesday" for heaven's sake. But I do think that if you are over the age of 21, you are better off being given a little warning.

I checked this with a whole rake of people – not just ones of like minds.

One woman said she hated the surprise for the first half hour. She felt the thing was too lavish, she had always let her cousins think they lived a much more modest lifestyle, she was in agony in case her in-laws might be staying in the house which was in no way tidy, she feared they had forgotten a neighbour who would take eternal umbrage.

But gradually the sense of delight that all these people thought her worthy of a celebration took over. She felt important and the centre of something. She had short over-excited conversations with people. Someone had made her an album of greetings and snaps. It's all bathed in a rosy delight, something she would never have had the arrogance to organise for herself. Yes, she says, surprises are great.

A man said he didn't really like his surprise party because his workmates had nothing to say to his golf-mates who had nothing to say to his pub-mates and it had cost too much.

Being able to guess the response is a large part of the surprise party culture. There is the optimistic belief that the recipient will allow gratitude and celebration to cover shock and the business of not being in control. I think you need to be a fairly intuitive psychologist, with a record of reading people's wishes very well, before you set a surprise in motion. While there can hardly be anyone who would not rejoice in a surprise gift or card, there must be many more for whom the wince factor of the sudden appearance of an unselected group of people would be too nightmarish to inspire a generous, grateful response.

MORNING AFTER

"She is praying that the guards were called to the party after she left, in answer to the complaints about the noise level"

This woman went to a party on Wednesday and she doesn't remember coming home. This is not a regular occurrence. In fact, it has never happened to her before. She was on a diet and didn't know very many people at the party. Out of nerves, she drank a lot more than she would usually drink and because she hadn't eaten, well, it must have all gone straight to her head.

There were lots of good things about the evening, like

the fact that she didn't drive home. Like she didn't appear to have been sick anywhere. Like she didn't bring anyone home with her. This was not totally clear to her, however, in the early hours of the morning. She thought she must have brought the taxi driver in with her because she saw him lying half in and half out of his side of the bed. But it turned out to be her coat, so that was a huge relief.

And she examined her eyes. They were, of course, red with drink but it didn't look as if they were swollen with tears or anything, so she thinks she may not have sat down and cried publicly about the particularly bad behaviour of a certain rat in her life. Her clothes, though distributed wildly around the house, were not torn, so she didn't wrestle with anyone. Her money and credit cards were intact. She hardly went to Leeson Street to bop the night away, buying wine for strangers.

In the absolute depths of alcoholic remorse, she was determined to explore all mitigating factors and find some signs of optimism, so she lists these very positively as proof that Things Could Have Been Worse.

Because she does not move in a crowd of screaming drunks who would meet for the cure the following day and make a half-hearted effort to fill in the missing parts of the jigsaw, she is totally at sea.

She doesn't know whether to apologise profusely to her hosts, find out who took her home, tell them some lies about being on medication which reacted badly with the minimal amount of alcohol she had, or to say nothing.

Perhaps she looked perfectly fine. Maybe everyone else had been down on their hands and knees barking like dogs and she had looked cool and distant and superior in the melee. Maybe her hosts were embarrassed that she had witnessed such bad behaviour.

Like all of us, she has been weary of people who keep saying they were drunk and making a thing about it. The man who says: "I know I've had a few drinks but . . ." The woman who says: "There I go, slurring my words."

Years ago, we all used to have a friend who was no drunker than any of us but who used to send a bunch of carnations with a note of apology after every gathering. It made us all think he was totally out of control. In fact, someone once asked him if he could send the flowers *before* the next party as it would save his hostess having to buy flowers.

And I have an American friend who says, after every single party he was ever at: "I'm afraid I was so drunk last night I was no addition to the scene." On no occasion has he been anything other than articulate and charming, and it is an eternal mystery why he claims he doesn't remember anything he said or did.

So back to the woman who got drunk on Wednesday. Should she join the ranks of the apologisers, or should she go along blithely assuming that everything was fine?

She knows quite a few people of the latter category – the non-apologetic sort. People who never mention the fact that they insulted you or spilled drink down your front or danced a hornpipe when other people were trying to have a normal conversation.

From time to time in Dublin, I see a woman who once told me that she had seen a documentary about yaks and every one of them reminded her of me. She told me this with her face dissolved in drink so that none of her features remained in the correct place. I think I would have preferred if, at a later date, she had said: "I'm afraid I was very peculiar the other night and I'm asking for a general absolution from everyone I spoke to." It would certainly make me feel a lot happier whenever the image of a yak comes into my mind. Otherwise, we have to assume (a) that she doesn't know she said this; (b) that she knows it and hopes I have forgotten it; or (c) that she meant it.

The woman who got drunk on Wednesday evening crawled around to the house and retrieved her car the following evening. She is in deep depression and in a lather of indecision. She is recalling every article she ever read which begged the question: "Are you an alcoholic?" She is searching desperately for someone who will tell her that it wasn't really a blackout, not a blackout as such. She is praying that the guards were called to the party after she left, in answer to complaints about the noise level.

I would advise her to apologise. As she left the party without her car, I'd think it was pretty clear that someone had agreed to take her home or at least made sure that she got home safely. That has to be acknowledged. You cannot take for granted that you can fall to bits in someone's house and that everyone else will look after you.

She doesn't have to tell the story of the diet, the empty calories, the dirty rat who treated her wrong, the fact that she thought her coat was perhaps the taxi driver. All she need say is that she has only now recovered from her ferocious hangover and would like to thank them for everything. She can leave lots of pauses where they can fill in the things she is thanking them for – no self-flagellation but some acknowledgement that all was not as it might have been.

There's an aggressive, macho charm about being the kind who never apologises and never explains. But it could mean you never get asked anywhere again, and are never given the opportunity to bring such principles into play.

LATE IN LIFE

"We should never again say to latecomers that they're in perfect time when the meal is stuck to the roof of the oven and the other guests are legless with pre-dinner drinks"

I regard people who say they'll meet you at 8 p.m. and then turn up at 8.30 as liars. I had a colleague, years ago in my teaching days, who used to smile and say that she was always late, as if it were something outside her control, like having freckles or a Gemini star sign. At first I went through agonies thinking she had been mown down by a bus. After that I would arrange to meet her, not on the corner of a street or at the cinema, but in a café where at least I could sit down while waiting. After that I stopped meeting her. There were too many main features beginning at 5.20 missed, too many buses gone, too many houses where I had to be part of an apology for an unpunctuality that was none of my making.

She lives in another country now and I met someone who had been to see her. Just as nice as ever, apparently, just as good company. Much loved by her children but treated as a dotty old lady who can't be relied on. She would never turn up to pick them up from school, so they just adapted to doing their homework in the school-yard. So she is still at it, thinking she can say one thing and do another, and everyone will forgive her because she is unpunctual the way other people are left-handed or colour-blind.

Of course she got away with it because people are so astounded by the unpunctual that they forgive them and allow them to roam the world as ordinary people instead of as the liars they are. It's our fault for putting up with it in every walk of life, and I advise people to declare war on the unpunctual. It's no longer acceptable to consider it an attractive, laid-back, national characteristic. It is, in fact, a lazy self-indulgent, discourteous way of going on. Already there are a lot of signs that people do not accept it as charming.

I remember a time when the curtain never went up on time in a Dublin theatre because, as the theory went, the Irish were all so busy being witty and wonderful and entertaining in bars they couldn't do anything as pen-pushing, meticulous and prosaic as coming in and being seated before eight o'clock. But enough protests from those who objected to people shuffling in late to performances have led to their not being admitted until the first interval, and it's very interesting to see how that has concentrated the ability to get to the place before the lights go out.

Staff of Aer Lingus don't think it's charming and witty to leave late because their wonderful free-spirited clients can't be hurried. Likewise with trains, the DART and the buses. Religious services don't take account of some quirk in the national psyche by having Mass at around 11 or Matins at approximately 10. Races, football matches, television programmes start on time. Why should business appointments and social engagements be let off this hook? And yet this week I was talking to an American publisher on the phone who said that she was expecting an Irish author in her office but he was 40 minutes late. She laughed good-naturedly and, even though she was 3,000 miles away,

I could see her shrug forgivingly. "Oh well, that's the Irish for you!" she said, as if somehow it explained something. To me it explained nothing.

As a race we are not naturally discourteous. In fact, if anything, we wish to please a bit too much. That's part of our national image. So where does this unpunctuality come into the stereotype? Has it something to do with being feckless and free and not seeing ourselves ever as a slave to any time-servers or time-keepers? It's a bit fancy and I don't think that it's at all part of what we are.

Not turning up at the time you promised seems quite out of character and, if we do it, it must be because it has been considered acceptable for too long. If nobody were to wait for the latecomer, then things would surely change. If the unpunctual were to be left looking forlorn and foolish when they had ratted on their promise, then people would keep better time. We shouldn't go on saying that it's perfectly all right and, nonsense, they mustn't worry, and really it was quite pleasant waiting here alone wondering was it the right day, the right place, or the right time. We should never again say to latecomers that they're in perfect time when the meal is stuck to the roof of the oven and the other guests are legless with pre-dinner drinks.

Sit in any restaurant, bar or hotel foyer and listen while people greet each other. "I'm very sorry. The traffic was terrible." "I'm sorry for being late. I couldn't get parking . . ." "I'm sorry. Are you here long? I wasn't sure whether you said one or half past . . . " "I'm sorry, but better late than never".

I wouldn't forgive any of these things. In a city, people with eyes in their heads know that the traffic is terrible; they can see it. Unless they have been living for a while on the planet Mars, they're aware that it's impossible to park. If they couldn't remember whether you said one or half past, that shows *great* interest in the meeting in the first place. And as for better late than never, I'm not convinced.

PIECES OF SILVER

"Inheritance, sentimental attachment, beautiful craftwork, valuable asset . . . it's no life for a piece of silver"

It's important that you know that this woman is not one of the Very Rich. She said I could write about her but I must say that her husband is a teacher and she works part-time in a dress shop. They have three children in their teens, they have one car, and pay a £200-a-month mortgage on their house.

Every July they go for three weeks to the seaside; they're off today and, when I met her, she was on her way into the bank to leave in the silver.

It was in a carrier bag, all polished up, and each piece wrapped carefully in soft cloths. She had been doing this as long as she could remember, taking it to the bank for three weeks a year.

She didn't know how much it was worth, but there were cream jugs and sugar basins and a teapot and salt cellars and a bon-bon dish. Maybe worth £2,000 or more.

They were mainly 1940s pieces, which her parents had received as wedding presents, and a few pieces from the 1970s, such as spoons which had been her own wedding presents. She clutched the bag as if she were expecting we would be felled to the ground by a bandit before she was able to pass it across the counter.

And, for the other 49 weeks of the year, did they use the

silver, pour milk from the jug, spoon salt from the salt cellar, eat old-fashioned humbugs or fruit pastilles from the bon-bon dish?

Was I mad or something? Of course they didn't.

Well, were the pieces of silver all nicely displayed at home and winking at them from a shelf, or even from behind glass doors, so they could see them and get pleasure from the shape of them and the way they looked if they weren't going to be allowed to be pressed into service?

Did I live in the real world or where? Of course they weren't displayed. Displayed, like an invitation to a burglar, like a notice saying "Look, here are the valuables." Well, where were they when they weren't in the bank for their holidays?

They were in a drawer behind the tea cloths, that's where they were. And did they ever get out at all? Well, the pair didn't entertain much, but suppose there was some kind of a do . . . but not always, they didn't want to be showing off, loading a table down with silver. It looked like boasting. It said "if you have it, flaunt it". That wasn't good.

But was it good, I asked, to be in the situation that you have to hide it behind the tea towels? And then, if you still have it, lug it to the bank for three weeks in July? Now we were squaring up for the fight.

So what would *you* do with it, she asked, not unreasonably. As it happens I had exactly the same kind of silver. A share of the pieces that had belonged to my parents, all of it 1930s Birmingham for some reason; maybe that's what they saved up for then.

Anyway, I used it non-stop, even to the extent of planting an African violet in one of the sugar bowls, because you couldn't use two sugar bowls at the same time. And people were always shaking their heads and saying it was criminal to use good silver like that, and not respecting it. But I liked it and I thought using it *was* respecting it. Like having your Solpadeine from a Waterford glass, if you have one, seems to be the right thing to do rather than making a value judgement and wondering would the glass violently object to being used for such humdrum purposes.

In the end I didn't keep the silver, because everyone was making such a fuss about it. We travelled so much, they said, it was inviting disaster to have it around the place and I was not going to beat a path up and down to the bank. What was the point of it if it was in a sports bag wrapped up in the dark? Someone should be looking at it and pouring things out of it.

I sold some in order to help with the house deposit, and 1 gave the rest away to the people I was going to give it to anyway in my will. They all said that, as usual, I was overdoing it and overreacting. But to me it was great.

Now I can see the silver when I go to their houses, and I don't care if they have to remember to get it back or burrow in the tea towel drawer for it, and I don't care whether they hate dirtying it up by putting milk and sugar and salt and pepper into it instead of leaving it in a sports bag. That's what it was made for.

So I was in a fine position to argue with the woman in the bank. But she was a spirited person. She said that this was her inheritance in the sense that it had been left to her, not in the sense that it was worth a fortune. She felt a sense of duty to hand it on to the next generation.

And, no, she didn't mind if they sold it when it came to their turn, or gave it away or used it to plant African violets in. That was their decision to make. And so, in front of my eyes, the silver went into a vault. To live a further lonely unseen life. Out of the tea towels and into the strong room.

Better by far than out of your house and into the meltdown or No-Questions-Asked gift trade, the woman said. The bank official joined in the discussion to say that quite a lot of people availed of their services. "There are people who value their silver," he said very disapprovingly.

Yes, and there are banks who value the possibility of renting out space to the nervous, I said.

It doesn't cost very much, the bank man said: £10 a year for an envelope, £20 a year for a grip bag.

Plus VAT? I wondered. Plus VAT he agreed. It was an animated discussion, and none of us changed our views. Inheritance, sentimental attachment, beautiful craftwork, valuable asset . . . it's no life for a piece of silver or your own peace of mind if it is going to be spent in the dark. Look at it or offload it.

She thinks everyone will agree with her, but I *know* they will agree with me.

Where There's Smoke

"I begged her to remember reading about the days when people used to pee into things under the table to save themselves the trouble of getting up and leaving the conversation . . ."

It's bad luck but it's true. It just sort of happened that smoking became unacceptable. And it's very bad luck on a friend of mine who says that she knows I, at least, will be sympathetic.

I who wheezed and coughed and hawked with her over the years across people's dining tables, over their new-born babies, in their brand new cars. Surely, just because I gave them up in some kind of act of foolish and public bravado, I haven't forgotten the compadres of the ashtray?

Surely I'm not going to join a bandwagon spouting the politics of hate, and start laying down rules about where and when she can smoke in my presence? She says that cured alcoholics don't go round shouting at other people who still drink: joggers don't take you by the throat and force you into a tracksuit. But the bad news is that I am . . . on the bandwagon. If it were her liver she was punishing with daily downpourings of Red Biddy, then it's her liver, not mine. If a jogger sees a non-jogger, then, selfishly, the jogger can leave the non-jogger be, sitting festering, getting fat and unfit. But if it's a smoker, then it's my air and my lungs that they are coming at and, for that reason alone, I think they have to face the fact that people are not cranks, weirdoes and freaks if they don't want to be in their company.

Now this woman has just become a grandmother and the whole joy of having the beautiful baby to play with has been marred by the new findings which seem to prove that even a grandmother having smoked might weaken the health of the child. She is trailing this guilt and the child is only six weeks old. When the baby was born the parents were congratulating themselves on being non-smokers but with this *statistic* – and she speaks in heavy italics – their faces have grown glum and disapproving and they are looking at her as if she has contributed leprosy to the genes of her first grandchild.

She came to tell me about it, and how grossly unfair and hurtful it was, but she lit a cigarette in the car and I literally can't bear people to smoke in it. So, in order to be kind, I stopped the car and we sat freezing on a beach, looking at the sea while she told me how rotten her daughter and her son-in-law were being and, for God's sake, everyone smoked until recently. The whole thing was just a media-inspired, holier-than-thou bit of hypochondria, she said, and by the time her granddaughter was old enough to hate and despise her smoking granny, there would be a revisionist school of thought that said tobacco cleared the tubes to your heart or stopped athlete's foot and everyone would be searching for it.

And then she said that we would both have hypothermia, so why didn't we get into the nice warm car. And I told her that I was such a bad driver that if anyone smoked in the car – and I started to cough or anything – I would probably plough headlong into the traffic coming the other way and we'd both go for the chop, and what her granddaughter thought of her would be irrelevant.

She looked at me thoughtfully and said I was much calmer when I smoked, had less fantasies, a lower level of anxiety and wasn't it a pity I was so doctrinaire. So I told her the truth. I said the smell of tobacco in a confined space really did make me feel sick and that the thought of emptying a car ashtray would turn my stomach.

She couldn't have been more insulted. I was the last person she would have expected to follow the crowd. Where were all the libertarian principles of long ago about living and letting other people live? But I said to her that in wild west films you saw people spitting all the time, getting up a huge throatful of spit and hurling it out of the side of their mouths on the floor. And even in old-fashioned gentlemen's clubs, they had a horrific thing called a cuspidor which people spat into.

And I begged her to remember reading about the days when people used to pee into things under the table to save themselves the trouble of getting up and leaving the conversation and the general conviviality of it all. Even among the most enthusiastic diners-out, you don't hear much of a call to re-introduce that practice.

And it's not only because the world had moved on from believing that there is one kind of person who would fill a cuspidor or a thing under the table and another sort of a person who would empty it . . . it's just because we don't want to accept unpleasant things if we don't have to.

If you add the belief that passive smoking is now considered a fact, then the poor smoker really is beleaguered.

No longer can we even look at the smokers indulgently and think of them as glamorous if suicidal figures, old-fashioned throwbacks to the black-and-white movie years, rotting their lungs and moving in a haze towards an early grave. Now they are dragging the rest of us to the grave with them and if people even partially believe this then a smoker is going to be as much fun at a gathering as an old man with a long beard and a scythe.

And also they smell awful.

In Georgie Best's gorgeous days, when he did that ad saying, "I'd never kiss a girl who smoked", it made a lot of girls think for a bit. It was one of the most successful anti-smoking campaigns ever run. If you go to a restaurant where there is a lot of smoking, your own coat smells terrible later. I don't think smokers should be attacked for the past; my friend should not be blamed for whatever weaknesses her granddaughter might inherit because, hand on heart, none of us knew. We really didn't.

But she should realise that it's disgusting and dangerous and, as such, you can't expect to make self-deprecating little jokes and say that you're afraid you're one of these awful endangered species, the Smoker, and expect people to pat you on the head, hand you an ashtray and allow you to pollute their atmosphere and their lungs.

I advised her to think in terms of belching and farting and spitting.

She said we could still be friends but would probably have long phone conversations or maybe one of us could go to prison and we could talk through a screen.

WEARY WORDS

"And if I was 25 years older than when last we met, so was she"

It was a lovely sunny day on Bloomsday and I was sitting in the hallway of the Joyce Centre in Dublin, delighted with myself. Why wouldn't I be? I was watching all the comings and goings, the people dressed up, the American tourists, the faces I hadn't seen for years. I was waiting to do an interview and was given a glass of lager to pass the time. Not many people would be having as good a time on a Thursday morning at 11.30 a.m., I said to myself.

And then a woman came in whom I used to know years ago, when we were young teachers. She was a very positive person then, I remember. She used to take her pupils on great trips to France, which they never forgot. She had amazing projects in her classroom, and she used to go around with a box on the back of her bicycle asking people who had gardens if she could have cuttings, and then she used to get the kids to plant them around the schoolyard.

She was a leader in everything, the first to give up smoking, the first to organise lunches where people were asked to contribute the price of a meal for the hungry, the first I knew to go to America for the summer and work as a camp counsellor. I had nothing but good memories of her. She seemed glad to see me too, but then her face fell. "You look desperately tired," she said sympathetically. "Are you all right?"

Well, the sun went out of the day and the fun went out of the Joyce Centre and the taste went out of the glass of lager and the sense of being as free as a bird went out the window. Tired is not a good thing to be told you look. Tired is terrible. And the really infuriating thing is that I was not tired, I had been in bed nice and early the night before. And I was tidy. Tired can often mean that you look like a tramp, but no, I had dressed up, complete with white collar, for the interview. And I wasn't sweating or collapsing up flights of stairs. I was sitting calm as anything in the hall. And if I was 25 years older than when we last met, so was she. So, stupid as this may seem, I looked upset. I must have bitten my lip or may have looked as if I was going to burst into tears, because she said at once that she was sorry, and wanted to know what she had said.

"I'm not tired," I said, like a big baby.

She tried to explain that tired was *okay*. We were entitled to be tired. By God, we had earned the right to it. We worked hard, we had done so much. It would be an insult if we *weren't* tired.

She was back-tracking, trying to dig herself out of it, I said.

No way, she insisted, and wasn't I the touchy one trying to read other words into a perfectly acceptable observation, and more meanings than were implied in an expression of concern?

But what was she going to do about my tiredness? Suppose I had admitted it? Just suppose I had agreed that I was flattened by fatigue and had been waiting for someone to come in that door to identify it. What was her cure? Had she ginseng or Mother's Little Helpers in her handbag? Did she have a personal fitness trainer, a protein diet, a Seventh Son or shares in a health farm?

We argued it away good-naturedly, as we had always argued in years gone by. She was always a woman of strong views, a characteristic I admire. I have even remembered many of her maxims, such as "Avoid restaurants that have strolling musicians", "Never play cards with a man named Doc" and "Don't resign before lunch".

But what's the point of telling someone that they look tired, even if you don't mean it as a euphemism for old, ugly, unkempt or rapidly going downhill? Was it a kind of sympathetic come-on . . . expecting an answer along the lines of Nobody Knows The Trouble I've Seen?

She was spirited about it. And she nearly won the argument. Would I prefer, she wondered, if we were all to turn into those dinkleberries who greet each other with an effusion of insincere compliments: "Oooh, you look marvellous" and "Oooh, you've lost loads of weight and honestly, I never saw you looking better, what *have* you been doing?" – the greetings and the compliments becoming like a ritual dance where the vain and the self-centred rake through a form of words, wondering if there is a "marvellous" too few or an expression of astonishment not heightened enough. Surely we haven't reached this stage?

But then, when she said "tired", did she mean that as some sort of shorthand, to be a jovial punch on the shoulders between old mates, a kind of bonding between the worn out?

She thought about it.

She thinks she meant that she liked me from the old days, and it was good to see me again, and when she came upon me I had a serious expression on my face as if I had been talking to a woman about her late husband and maybe she remembered me roaring about, not sitting down. And in a sense, she didn't want to be one of those people who always said twitter-twitter things and assumed other people had lives that were free of care. And on reflection, she said, now that we had argued the thing down to the bone, she would never as long as she lived tell another human being that they looked tired again.

LINGUISTICALLY CHALLENGED

"It is much more lofty to correct someone's spelling if you have not been invited or paid to do so"

It was probably right of that nice mild man who has been married to Margaret Thatcher for years to correct her when she got the name of the country she was in wrong. She was praising warmly the people, parliament and customs of one Far Eastern country when in fact she was in another, one which hadn't had entirely cordial relations with the other for some centuries. Dennis cleared his throat and put her right.

I imagine that, when she took off her shoes and calmed down her hair and looked back on yet another bone-achingly tiring night, she might have been grateful. Suppose she had gone on mixing up Indonesia and the Philippines all night, the hatchets and the tumbrels might have come out for her even sooner than they eventually did. Also, he did it nicely. As if he weren't entirely sure himself, but was taking the risk.

I thought of him last week in Manchester when a nervous young woman was trying to chat with her new in-laws. They were all in a big, somewhat anxious-making hotel lobby. It was the kind of place where you might expect a heavenly choir to come out of the woodwork. And I had already travelled down in the lift with Barry Manilow.

Anyway, the girl was trying too hard, her dress was too short, too shiny, her heels too high, too uncertain, her tone too screechy for the dowdy and slightly supercilious clan into which she had married.

Her young husband obviously loved her to bits. He had his arm protectively under her elbow to guide her through the minefields of slippy floors and dangerous conversations.

She was telling the in-laws their holiday plans. "Jim's booked us two weeks in a commodium," she said excitedly. Her husband would have liked the marble floors and the brass rails to part and deliver them inside the earth's crust. "I think you mean condominium, love," he said.

Her face was scarlet.

"Isn't that what I said?" she managed.

"Well, sort of." He didn't really mean to but he did sort of smile a bit apologetically towards his mother and father and sister. I wanted to cry.

It's a meaningless word. It's a word anyone would pause over, wondering if by any chance you had said condom instead. It's a made-up word coming from American culture, not ours. It has some technical meaning in the US, meaning you own it more than people in apartments own theirs, or on a different kind of lease.

Why should any of us have to know that kind of a word just because it has become travel-agent speak? I remember Terry Wogan saying he had a friend who owned a condominium who always referred to it as a pandemonium, because he thought that's what it was actually called.

I longed to tell this girl this, but they take you away firmly from hotel foyers if you butt into other people's lives with stories like that.

What should that nice boy, who didn't intend to make little of his young wife, have done?

He could have talked about the advantages of condominiums or whatever, showing that he knew the word and maybe she would pick it up. Or he needn't even have done that. They weren't out to catch her, he only embarrassed everyone by the correction.

Would he have corrected a colleague, a friend, a stranger even? The women I had dinner with, booksellers, did not agree with me. They said, if they had said the wrong word, they would prefer to be corrected, then they would not make the same mistake again. Surely I as a teacher would go down that route?

If they pronounced the name of an author or a book title wrongly, they would prefer to be told, they said. That way they wouldn't allow a conspiracy of pity to grow up around them, pigeon-holing them as people less than they were. All of which could be avoided by a simple correction.

But in public? Yes, they shrugged, they were young, they were on the way up a career ladder, they didn't want to be held back by not being able to pronounce Anouilh on the rare occasions that anyone might want one of his works.

They told embarrassed stories of how colleagues thought that Carson McCullers was a man, or that *My Secret Garden*, a sexual fantasy book, was in fact a work of horticulture. How much better to have been told. The public embarrassment took 10 seconds and was then over.

I admired their courageous attitude but think that they might be over-optimistic about the thickness of their skins. And, of course, once you start going along some line of thought, there are dozens of examples to illustrate it.

The young trainee in the next hotel showed me the bathroom, and pointed out bath, shower, lavatory and duvet. Was I going to tell him it was a bidet? No, I damn well wasn't. I don't care if he takes longer to make general manager of the chain; he was a kid. I was not going to tell him one nouveau, poncey word from another.

I have had many letters from youngsters wanting to "persue" a career in journalism and I've let them "persue" it on the grounds that there is a spell check on most word processors and by the time they get there they might have learned how to spell it. Is this a lofty patrician attitude, a patronising tolerance of the lower orders? I don't think so, truly I believe it is much more lofty to correct someone's spelling if you have not been invited or paid to do so.

I have never corrected the numerous English people who pronounce my home town of Dalkey as if the L were not silent, because I surely have pronounced their home towns incorrectly too, and it doesn't really matter. What would matter is to be called up short in front of someone and given a more acceptable pronunciation for a word that had just left your mouth innocently, when you thought it was fine.

Like the people in our road in London who know exactly what a woman means when she says that two nice people from the Johanna Hovises called. Very polite and asking you about being saved. Everyone knows she means Jehovah's

Witnesses; what a pedantic down-putting world it would be if anyone were ever to correct her.

HOUSE PRIVATE

"For some reason, they got locked into the phrase. They thought, in their grief, that it had some dignity instead of working out what it meant"

Some months ago I saw a death notice in the paper. It was the father of a woman I know. He was a man in his seventies, popular, respected, he liked his work. After his retirement he was known in his neighbourhood and much visited by friends.

Then I noticed the words House Private at the end of the announcement. It struck me as an odd thing to say in the circumstances. It wasn't as if there was anyone else in the house who was sick or frail, someone to whom visitors or callers would be a nightmare.

His death had been a peaceful happening after some weeks' illness, so there was no question of it being a suicide, a tragic motor accident or some drama that might have attracted the appalling gawpers.

He was not a well-known celebrity whose house might have been invaded by paparazzi or sightseers, coming in the guise of mourners – if such a thing ever happens, which in this land is not really likely.

They are a loving, warm family; they didn't want to refuse access to their house on the day of a funeral because they would all be at each other's throats and wanted to have their blood-letting in private. These are generous people who would be delighted to dispense drink and sandwiches; they were not trying to avoid putting their hands in their pockets to buy a beverage for those who came to sympathise over their father.

They are articulate and outgoing: it's not as if they would be struck dumb by any emotional scene or the show of warmth by neighbours, colleagues, extended family and friends.

They must have been to enough funerals in their lives to know how consoled and pleased a family always seems when others come to mark the occasion and show that they cared about the person who died and those who survived him.

The more I saw the words, the more I wondered whether they meant that the removal to the church and the actual Requiem Mass were also private. Would it be an intrusion to go to those? But no, the paper had given the times, so they must be expecting people to turn up on these public occasions. So I went.

And a small, sparse group of people stood in a Dublin city church on an autumn evening waiting for the funeral party to arrive. It was a very small group, when you considered what kind of man was going to be buried the next day.

One of my friends didn't come with me; she said that when it said House Private it really meant Funeral Private. She said we would be in the way.

The very short line of sympathisers went up and shook hands with the family.

"Please come back to the house," the woman I know said.

"No, no, it says House Private," I said.

"It doesn't mean you, PLEASE come, there's hardly anyone here," she said with a different kind of tears in her eyes now, tears that her kind, gregarious father was not being given the send-off he deserved.

So I went to the house where they had glasses ready and bottles, and rooms cleared to receive people and plates of things covered in cling-film in the kitchen. And it was very sad, not just because he was dead and they had lost their father, but because, inadvertently, they had sent out the wrong signal and given him the wrong farewell.

It was hard to know whether you were making it better or worse by saying that people might have been kept at a distance by the House Private. I thought it might explain why the doorbell wasn't ringing. This was the first funeral that the family had had to organise; their mother had died many years ago, long before they were old enough to be involved in the arrangements.

"I don't know why we put that in the paper," the woman I know said.

"We must have had some reason," her sister said. They had regarded it as some part of a formula, one of the things that happened at this odd, unreal time, something they saw other people put in the paper, like Rest in Peace. They hadn't thought about it at all.

It's many months later. The woman wrote to me and suggested I use her example for this column. She said there must be many other people who might learn from this, might just pause before they fell into a form of words and made a gesture which was regarded by some as snobbish, as if they were excluding those who might come to the house, those who would not have been entertained in the normal course of events. This was what grieved her most.

Also, she said that the funeral director *had* asked them twice if they really wanted the house to be private; he had said that sometimes it was a comfort to have the presence of friends and that we were lucky in Ireland where we had the vocabulary of sympathy, unlike other cultures where death was treated as a personal sorrow to be endured and recovered from in private. But for some reason they got locked into the phrase. They thought, in their grief, that it had some dignity, instead of working out what it meant.

If all his friends had been there it would not have been a grotesque Irish wake, a roaring party with people forgetting the reason for their gathering; it would have been something that might have given them strength and banished the bleakness of the time.

There may well be good and sensitive reasons for saying House Private but she urged me to advise those who do so, merely from some sense of thinking it the Right Thing, to ask themselves who they are shutting out and why.

Advance Planning

"Making an arrangement in advance to meet friends is truly not a sign that we have arrived in a yuppie culture dictated by slamming filofaxes down on tables"

I was at a friend's house recently, partly to set something up in aid of a charity and partly to have a great chat. There we were at the kitchen table when there was a knock on the door. It was a neighbour who had called in for a chat. She was a very nice woman and her chat was perfectly pleasant and, if she had been invited in, I would have been delighted to meet her. But because she had just dropped in I thought it spoiled everything. The fund-raising idea was left up in the air and the marvellous stories were half-finished because you wouldn't try to bring a stranger up to date on the whole cast of characters involved.

The neighbour had a telephone but she hadn't thought to ring. "I just took the chance that you'd be in," she said with a beaming smile, and down she sat.

Eventually I left before her, with a great sense of dissatisfaction and frustration and also with some self-doubt. Was it perhaps churlish to resent someone calling uninvited? Not at all. I deeply resent it. I wouldn't do it to anyone and I wouldn't want anyone to do it to me.

My friend rang the next day to apologise. "I'm so sorry," she wailed, "but what on earth could I do? I couldn't tell her not to come in when she had arrived on the doorstep, could I? I had to make her a cup of coffee too, didn't I?"

I think not.

She could have said: "Listen, come in and say hello for a minute, but Maeve and I are doing some work and we honestly have to get on with it or it will never be done." That was true. Well, 80 per cent true. The neighbour was a reasonable and intelligent woman; she wouldn't think a door was being slammed in her face. And it would have been a perfectly courteous way to ask her not to make a night of it. We had papers and lists out on the table.

I honestly think that the hostess was to blame just as much as the woman who came in. After all, if people crow with delight that it's lovely to see you, even when it isn't, how are you to know that it's an awkward time and you are not at all the welcome guest that they keep insisting you are?

But, my friend would say, that's a very Dublin attitude. It's not what people do in the country; they are much more casual there. In the country, the art of friendship and calling to see one another hasn't fallen away.

Excuse me a moment. So where do we live?

Exactly, we live in Dublin. So I think we need not apologise for doing things in a Dublin way, even if that is meant to be some kind of a swipe at Dubliners for being ungracious fortress-holders who hate unlocking their ramparts.

And I bet you anything that in the country they don't light up with joy at the sight of an uninvited guest bowling along through the green fields or across the mountain passes. No one is going to convince me that our rural friends are going to be dewy-eyed with delight when they see a couple of bores, or even nice people who have time on their hands, arriving unexpectedly at the door.

Making an arrangement in advance to meet friends is truly not a sign that we have arrived in a yuppie culture dictated by slamming filofaxes down on tables and checking dates like tycoons. I am delighted if someone writes or rings and says he or she will be in the area and what about a drink or a meeting.

Delighted. And then I regard it as a highpoint of the day and get all my work finished for a spurious deadline. On the other hand, I am enraged if I am with someone I haven't seen for a long time and there is a knock or ring at the door.

So why not ignore it, you might ask? The world is divided into those who can let a phone ring without answering it and those who cannot. And what kind of atmosphere do you have if you are cowering in your own house while someone is belting at the door?

The young just love the adventure and the excitement of the Unknown in the ring of a doorbell. It could be their Future waiting out there. The rest of us find little joy in the appearance of someone who was Just Passing or who was Wondering How We Were. It's a sign of age, I suppose, maturity – the realisation that there aren't unlimited years left of visiting people and being visited, and you want to do it right.

It's a question of experience, too. One casual dropper-in I know was cured when he went to a house where there was a huge argument in progress and bad feeling hung like ectoplasm at shoulder level around the place. Then he went to a house where they were having a supper party and almost all his friends were there, so everyone was mortified.

He gave up dropping in unexpectedly when he went to see his aunt and uncle on a Sunday afternoon and got the distinct impression they had been summoned from a connubial bed to answer the door. His own view, that they were much too old for that sort of thing anyway and if it had been wild and wonderful they wouldn't have answered the door, was not credited by any of us as satisfactory. He telephones nowadays and is a much more welcome guest.

It's not just the high fliers, the decision-makers, the self-conscious superwomen who can't bear to be discovered unawares: it's the people who have decided to take out the contents of all the kitchen drawers and sort them; the workers who are terminally tired and are dozing in front of the television. It's the parents who have decided to spend proper time with their children; the couples who have made a bit of time to talk about a holiday; the woman who is just getting to like her sisters-in-law; the man who has decided to touch up the hair at his temples with a little dark colour; the mother whose baby has finally gone to sleep; the old people who hate answering the door after dark; the person who has just thought how peaceful this is . . . a good book, a nice dog asleep by the fire and a hot whiskey. Those are the kind of people you are interrupting when you call unannounced, and, unless you are as entertaining as Peter Ustinov, I advise you to think very carefully before you ring that doorbell.

RASH DECISIONS

"I'd prefer to have roast cocker spaniel than rabbit, but people don't serve it very often so there is hardly a regular confrontation . . ."

When this couple accepted an invitation to go out to dinner last week, the wife did not say beforehand that spicy food brings her face out in blotches and her husband did not say that fish has always reminded him of cod-liver oil ever since his days in boarding school and that he literally can't swallow it.

Now the reason they didn't mention these two facts was because they did not want to sound like guests from the funny farm, finicky, faddish and laying down the law about what they were going to eat when they arrived at someone else's table. But they were served a fish starter and, as everyone else was devouring it, he pushed it around his plate wishing there was even a lettuce leaf to hide it under, wishing there was a paper napkin he could wrap it up in like he used to do at school, wishing that he didn't feel like gagging every time he brought it up to his mouth.

Eventually his wife came to his rescue and told a funny story about how mad we are to think of fish as a penitential dish and doesn't it really show your age . . . And everyone took it in their stride, except for the woman who had prepared the meal, who said in a slightly aggrieved way: "But you should have said. I'd have made you something different."

That was the first course.

In came the main course. A dish of chicken done with ginger and cardamom and garlic. The woman who had just managed a reprieve for her husband and saved him from having to eat a fillet of plaice looked in horror as the spicy dish was served onto her plate. As a couple they had already commanded enough attention as fusspots, she thought, and the conversation had moved on to happier channels.

She looked sadly at the plate in front of her and decided to go ahead and get blotches. First her neck reddened then the bits in front of her ears. She could feel the heat of the rash. Twice she saw her husband try to explain and twice she shook her head.

By the end of the evening, several people asked if she was feeling all right. Flushed and itchy, she looked as if she had an unpleasant rash, aggravated perhaps by drink.

She said there was nothing she could have done. You can't turn yourself into some kind of self-regarding hypochondriac and go about listing the foods you find unacceptable, not when it's hospitality that is being offered in someone else's home, she said. She agreed that, if she was a vegetarian, then she would say so in advance but she thinks it would be pretentious to mention the two kinds of food that didn't agree with them. Normal people are able to eat a little of everything and she and her husband are normal, even though they mightn't have shown too many signs of it on this particular occasion. She said that most of the time there wasn't a problem: people were going in more and more for buffets and more often than not you would be asked to help yourself. So the question of being faced with a plate of food you couldn't eat rarely occurred. On balance, she said, she would prefer to take the risk.

I think she is wrong. When you invite people to your house presumably it's because you like them and you want to feed them things they would like to eat rather than force them to eat their greens and their crusts and take spoonfuls of stuff that might even make them ill.

If you invite friends for a meal, it takes money to buy the food, time to cook it and you are hoping that it will all make for a successful evening. Wouldn't you much prefer someone to tell you casually what they couldn't or didn't want to eat in advance? There are ways of doing this – as a race we are not known to be short either of a word or the right words.

"All right," this woman said to me. "What would *you* do?"

Alas, in my case, I can eat anything, and have all the signs of it. The only thing I couldn't eat is rabbit. I'd prefer to have roast cocker spaniel than rabbit, but people don't serve it very often so there is hardly a regular confrontation between me and the bunnies.

Nowadays, however, people are using more oriental herbs and spices so it would be reasonable to expect things to have a more exotic flavour than in the more bland times of the past. The country has also become converted to fish, so it's almost an even bet that some sort of seafood will turn up.

To answer her question: what would I do?

I would put myself in the position of the woman who had cleaned her house, bought the food and prepared a meal for her friends. And I would not have wanted to see a friend push food around a plate like an enemy. And I would not have wanted to see another guest go purple with allergies in front of my eyes.

I would have been perfectly content with a short and undramatic explanation of the foods that did not suit. But I would have liked it in advance and then not have it referred to again.

If someone says they are on a diet and don't want big helpings, I think that is perfectly fair if they tell you quietly, but I think it is destructive and anti-celebratory if they say it like a Christian martyr during the meal and make everyone else feel guilty or gluttonous.

A friend of mine who is a caterer agrees with me, and says that Irish people can be uncharacteristically reticent about saying what they can't eat. She thinks it comes from a fear of being thought a crank or being seen to have pretensions which our grandparents wouldn't have had the luxury to entertain.

She does suggest, however, that if you plan to serve shellfish, that you should always offer an alternative, and leave it nearby so that your guests can choose a slice of melon as a replacement starter, say, or a large salad which would cover a main course. It is no trouble, she said, even at a formal dinner party, to prepare a special plate in advance. But it can create great trouble and disappointment when someone turns out to be not able to eat what you have prepared.

Airlines offer alternatives nowadays, so do caterers for functions and conferences – even at formal weddings, vegetarian dishes are available as a matter of course. So if exceptions can be made quite happily in public places among strangers, it seems odd to think that it would not be acceptable among friends.

PART II

PRINCIPLES AND PREJUDICES

Faith, Hope and . . .

"The danger would be that we become so watchful and politically correct in not falling for the con men that we may forget those who are relying on us . . ."

The woman in the red jacket did not have a closed mind. She wasn't a killjoy, or someone who wanted to write off any celebration of Christmas. She didn't have to go into intensive care if she saw Santa Claus in November, but she did draw the line at some things. And one of those things was charity Christmas cards.

She never sends them, she says, because only a fraction of what you pay for them goes to the cause. She says she knows this for a fact. And also, she doesn't like the feel of it. She says, it's like the people who used to ring bells and call a crowd if they were giving alms. Why didn't those who want to support a charity do so quietly, as in the case of the Widow's Mite, without drawing attention to it by sending a printed proof of their generosity to friends?

I didn't agree. I thought that if you *were* going to spend maybe 50 pence on a card, many times over, then why not let a portion of that go to help a cause? And the fact that the charity's name is printed on it isn't really boasting and braying and saying how good we are, it's reminding people of the charity in the most minimal way and possibly telling them of your commitment to it.

But the woman in the red jacket said that, although she accepted the purity of my motives, she felt it was a dangerous thing to do in many ways. Firstly, those of us who bought such cards were being conned because of the huge proportion that went to middlemen. Secondly, we might start feeling good and thinking that we had contributed in some significant way to a cause we believed in, whereas in fact we had only given a pittance.

The conversation was amicable and ended well. We both agreed to think about it.

To take just one charity of the many as an example, in my case I had already ordered my Christmas cards, as I always do, from the Irish Cancer Society, so I wasn't going to think about the issue very deeply. Because, though I claim to have a terrifically open mind, this is something I don't feel I will change my view about. But to be fair in terms of the discussion, I thought I'd ring and inquire how much of the money did go to the Irish Cancer Society, and how much got taken up along the way.

The Irish Cancer Society says that if you buy one of their cards through a shop, say for 50 pence, they will get 60 to 70 per cent of what you pay, in other words, 30-35 pence. Yes, they would get a higher percentage if you bought it directly from them, but they stress that they are more than happy to sell though the retail trade. They depend on it utterly to reach the great mass of people who go into shops to choose cards. They are happy to pay a percentage for the normal business of commerce and also to pay 21 per cent VAT. This is the way things are. It's not as if there are any nefarious middlemen out there, hawking them around and taking a huge amount off the top.

So how much sheer profit do they make from those of us who buy Irish Cancer Society Christmas cards? They make £75,000-£80,000 profit. It's very important to them, and, like many charities, they rely on it more and more heavily each year. They put this money into three areas, into research, into an education programme and into buying some badly needed hospital equipment for the diagnosis or treatment of cancer.

Their other big fund-raising effort is Daffodil Day and the money from that goes towards home-care services, night nurses and a freephone service. So it's all earmarked – what they do with it and what they need it for, this money raised by people buying a Christmas card with their name on it. They sounded greatly alarmed that anyone might cease to support any worthwhile charity out of fear of being conned or of being dubbed a public do-gooder.

I was fair to the woman in the red jacket in that I thought about it a lot. She had asked me if there were any kind of Christmas cards I didn't like, and there are. Open-minded tolerance doesn't have to be so bland and wishy-washy that you beam at every bit of cardboard you open. I resent the male chauvinist pigs who send feminist cards as a tee-hee joke. I don't like blasphemous cards or very big tasteful ones of buildings that nobody knows, or too many skating ladies on frozen lakes. But that's it.

I don't think any the less of anyone who is saving a whale or restoring the wing of some falling-down place. If my eye falls on the fact that someone's card will give 30 pence to the Samaritans, or to fight famine, or to house the homeless, then I am pleased rather than annoyed. I certainly wouldn't think that the sender wanted to be admired or praised for doing it.

Nor would I assume that they believed they had conquered the problem single-handed by placing the organisation on a sound financial footing. Thanks to television exposés and newspaper articles, we have been made aware of scams and false-hearted entrepreneurs who tug at our heart strings. The danger would be that we become so watchful and politically correct in not falling for the conmen that we may forget those who are relying on us at this time of year.

I advise people to buy a card in aid of charity. It's more important really than finding a tasteful print, and some of those cards which aid good causes have many a tasteful print in their repertoire anyway.

The £80,000 at Christmas that the Irish Cancer Society will get from those of us who buy their cards will be spent on things that matter. And, at this time of year, when I think of family and friends who have died of cancer and, much, much more positively, of family and friends who have lived with cancer and have been cured on account of the research, education programmes and equipment . . . then, to me, there's no better way of buying a greeting card.

STARKERS

"I would say group sex was as far from their minds as clog dancing"

She has a part-time job and they put all the money she earns in a kind of leisure fund. They buy the holiday from it and the music centre and the swinging seat for the garden. So this year they were looking through the brochures to decide where to go and her husband said he would really fancy two weeks on a naturist holiday. At first she thought this was looking at plants or wild life, then she realised that he didn't know B from a bull's foot about botany and what he was talking about was a nudist colony. That's what he wanted, to go to some awful place with sand dunes and little huts where everyone was naked 24 hours a day.

She was much disturbed by the brochure he had sent for. There was a lot of reference to "individual" cabins, and "family" cabins. What did that mean? On a normal holiday they didn't stress that you were going to have your own room in the hotel and not share it with any other couple who happened to be on the same package tour. Did this mean that you had the option of being an ordinary couple?

She wrote to me because her husband has gone mad and her friend has gone tight-lipped and maybe it's the kind of thing I might have a view on. She says she's 40 and quite ordinary, whatever that means. She has what she thought was a happy marriage; they have two children in their teens, children who have now outgrown the family holiday and want to be with their own friends, which is fine.

But was the norm group sex with people writhing away, all naked, all day and all night?

I was so flattered to be invited to get involved, rather than having to strain to hear what people were saying behind menus and in dark corners, that I wrote back immediately and asked her what her worst fear about the whole thing was and why her friend had become tight-lipped.

She wrote back. She didn't really want advice as such, just a view. In other words, I wasn't to make a federal case out of it. But her answers were as follows.

She was afraid he didn't love her anymore. If he did, why would he want to go and gawp at naked women? She was afraid they would look idiotic and no one would talk to them. Or that somehow, for some unfathomable reason, they would be so desirable that hundreds of Swedish and German and Belgian naturists would fancy them to bits and want to go to bed with them all day and all night. Or that they might meet someone from home.

Her friend just said that the man was having a mid-life crisis and he only brought the matter up in order to be reassured that he was the greatest. The friend said that these things occurred in a marriage and were best slapped down and not encouraged. And that it had all to do with too much explicit sex and violence on television anyway.

She ended her letter saying: "I know you were never in a nudist colony yourself but still you might have a view".

Wrong. Wrong. I *was* in a nudist colony myself, years ago in what they now call Former Yugoslavia. I was there for 14 hours and I advise her not to worry about a thing, to take no notice of the tight-lipped friend and to go with him.

It's only a bit of wobbly flesh. Once she gets over the shock of thinking "those people have come down to breakfast without their clothes," she'll settle down and enjoy it fine. Let's take her worries.

If he wants to gawp at naked women, it doesn't mean he doesn't love her any more and he can gawp at them anyway in magazines, on videos and at most resorts.

They won't look any more idiotic than anyone else. I was so mortified at *my* nudist colony that I used to sit on seats with my handbag on my lap, my arms crossed across my chest and my chin in my hand, pretending I was deep in thought and sending out lizard glances through my sun glasses to see what was passing by.

And what was passing by was immensely reassuring. Men with gigantic stomachs hanging over not little satin briefs, but sort of lost, inoffensive-looking appendages. No problem for anyone there. And women with tanned skin and pendulous breasts. And of course the usual quota of Miss Worlds and Mr Universes that you see anywhere, but they are no more jealous-making naked than they are semi-clothed.

Now I was there in the line of duty so I went round with a notebook, interviewing people. And I would say group sex was as far from their minds as clog dancing. Lots of them had little naked children by the hand, they all talked a lot about being free and they referred to people who wore clothes as "textiles". The people were textiles now, not the clothes.

It was very awkward eating meals; you would forget and let bits of hot food fall on you and somehow it seemed sort of awkward getting it off. And I used to stick to the chair. But that was all. If they met someone from home, well, then someone from home was there too, so no sweat.

On any holiday, people make compromises. For years I have seen women agree to go and watch a match on television; men agree to tour shops they find boring; friends go to the museums to please one and to the disco to please the other. We are kind to those we love and they to us; it's not the end of the world to go on one holiday that you don't fancy, to please someone you do. Next year she can choose.

The tight-lipped friend is another matter. The friend was no help to her at all. I advise this woman to tell her friend no more, to smile enigmatically and say "let's talk no more about holidays". And then she should go off and wobble and laugh with her husband in the naturist place and talk about silly old textiles, and being free, and remember to take lots of heavy duty sun cream for the bits that haven't been exposed for a while, and not to sit down on hot benches for fear of roasting her bum.

LIGHT UP AND LIVE

*"Today is Saturday and every time I hear a church bell ringing
I will think that it could have been his funeral Mass"*

It's great that he's still alive. Still sailing out of side roads
and lanes into the traffic. Still assuming that people who get
out of their cars, shake him, shout at him and then burst
into tears are just mad grown-ups. Seriously disturbed adults
thinking they own the world because they drive cars. It's
much better that he's alive and 13 and unrepentant than
dead in a mortuary, awaiting burial this morning.

His parents will go about whatever they do on a Saturday
morning; they will not be sitting stunned in a house,
waiting for the car to come and take them to the church.
His friends will be out with him whirling, swooping and
trick-acting on their cycles as usual, looking for adventure
and delighted to have wheels that might take them further
afield to find it.

You might pass him today, he'll be easier to see in the
daylight, just as slippery and eager to get where he is going,
with the same casual disregard for any rules of the road that
he had on Tuesday night. But when it gets dark you won't
see him. He'll be there all right, he's a grown-up of 13, he
doesn't have to be in at Lighting Up Time. He can stay out
way after nine, if his parents know where he is.

He will be heading home after dark in his fine dark
jacket, his near-black jeans, on a bicycle without a lamp,
without a rear light reflector, with no trace of luminous
paint, with no glowing belt, no white scarf, no helmet and

66

no worries. He will tell nobody about the near miss that he had on Tuesday night.

Who would he tell? Not his parents. They might darken their brows and sympathise with an unknown adult who had leaped from her car, shaken him, and then, with tears pouring down her face, assured him that he was only alive because she was driving at 25 miles an hour because it was raining. They might suggest buying some of these safety things like lamps and rear lights and they might cut short his wild and free cycling hours.

No, he wouldn't tell them. He wouldn't have thought it worth telling his mates. They're all sick of us finger-wagging adults, shaking our heads, peering with our weak eyes at perfectly visible things and then blaming them because we are too feeble to see them.

They wouldn't be interested in his brush with death, they've had it many a time. They tell the adult to chill out or get a life or, in the interests of speed, they say sure, yes, no problem, they'll get a light tomorrow and thanks, just to get rid of us so that we can shuffle off to whatever geriatric unit mistakenly allowed us out to drive.

He is 13 and has no imagination. He is lucky enough not to have *my* imagination. Today is Saturday and every time I hear a church bell ringing I will think that it could have been his funeral Mass; whatever his parents normally do on a Saturday morning they are doing only because I am a timid driver and terrified of the rain making things more difficult to see than they already are.

I can almost hear myself talking to them, telling them how sorry I was, how hard I tried to avoid him. I wouldn't even want to add to their grief by telling them that he was an irresponsible little devil, a danger to himself and others and that I was so much in the right it would make your head swim. Because their child would be dead and that is not the language to be used.

And there would be a picture of him on the mantelpiece and, for the rest of their lives, his brothers and sisters would wonder what he would have been like if he had grown up. And maybe his mother and father would have wondered, as the years went by, whether they could have done something more – like examined his bike every time he went out on it, or insisted that he wore reflective clothing if the little red light had come off the back.

Maybe they would. Or maybe they would have spent today, and the time that follows it, thinking about selfish motorists in big warm cars driving on a wet night and mowing down defenceless children. And there *are* many cases where parents are right to mourn and rage over children killed by drunks or speeders or even the preoccupied. But this would not have been one of them.

My fevered imagination can create scenes of family and friends trying to reassure me, trying to make me feel that there was nothing I could have done. I would think that I had taken up driving too late in life. Possibly, I would never get over the guilt.

So what is going to happen? I drive slowly already, I'm going to be a danger to other traffic after this. The boy? Is he kitted out in reflective gear, now astride a perfectly lit machine? Is he what? He thinks that because he sees the light of a car, the person in the car can see him.

I saved his life on Tuesday and I advise his parents to tell him that he is wrong. He is only 13 and he won't listen to anyone else. He won't listen to me – unstable, tearful and loud. He won't listen to the National Safety Council – gang of grown-ups, like school and the guards and everyone else, conspiring to prevent you having any kind of a life. But he *has* to listen to his parents just in order to have a bit of peace.

If they say: "You don't get on that bike again until you have proper lights and proper luminous strips" and if they mean it, then it's going to be such a hassle every time . . . he'll do it.

If his parents themselves wore a bit of fluorescent something on them, even if they were crossing the road to post a letter, he would see it as the norm, not as some kind of weakling nonsense, the hallmark of a nervous child instead of a daredevil grown-up which is what you are at 13.

At 13 you don't read statistics and, even if someone else reads them forcibly to you, you don't believe they apply to you. The latest figures the National Road Safety Council has for cyclists killed on our roads refer to 1992. That year 35 cyclists were killed; 136 were very seriously injured; 609 were just injured.

At 13 you wouldn't think about this, it would be just one more sad thing, like war and famine and things that happen in other places. But if I had a 13-year-old child who was intending to cycle anywhere tonight, I wouldn't care how much family aggro it caused, I'd dress him up like the Kish lighthouse. I'd have him looking like a Christmas tree if necessary – just so that he could be seen by the well-meaning folk as well as the drunks and the speeders who will undoubtedly be out this weekend as well.

IN LOCO PARENTIS

"Were they mad to let her have this fellow in her room? Were they mad if they made a scene about it?"

This woman is 47 and her best friend is also 47 and, long ago, went to live in America. The friend in America kept in touch – pictures of family, long Christmas letters, visits every three years when they came to Europe.

Then she wrote with a suggestion. Her daughter, who would be 17, would love to come to London for six months to do one of those posh secretarial courses that also involved grooming courses and learning how to arrange flowers. It would look awfully good when she came back to the States. It would give her confidence and smooth some of the rougher edges.

The friend in America said that the girl was very young and silly, and it would be a huge relief to her if she could stay in the London friend's house – as a paying guest.

The friend in America had read between the lines; she had realised that times were hard and cash was short, and that a paying guest would be just the thing. Especially an extrovert 17-year-old girl who would love everything and be a bit of a help around the house as well.

The London friend and her husband had no children, so they inquired well in advance what time the girl should come home in the evenings, whether she could travel on the Underground after dark and if they should offer her wine at meals. They didn't think about the one question which they needed to know how to answer.

The 17-year-old girl arrived. She was glowing with health and vitality and looked like an advertisement for orange juice and fibre. She had perfect manners and declared herself very pleased with London, her new home and her training course.

Eleven nights after she came to stay, she brought a boy home with her and took him to her room. The London friend and her husband were up all night, trying to think what to do. They could hardly knock on the girl's door and ask her to order the young man out of the house. Would they tell her in the morning that this occurrence must never happen again? Would they call the States and ask for guidance from her parents?

Were they being ridiculously old-fashioned and fuddy-duddy? Was this perhaps the way all young people carried on nowadays? Should they just check that she had been to the family planning clinic and practised safe sex? Would their obligation, and interest, end there?

If only they had been at home the previous evening, they could have indicated that it was not the expected thing for a guest to invite another guest to her room, but they had already told her that she was welcome to bring friends to the house. They had not meant male friends, to sleep.

So the dawn came, eventually, and they said nothing to the girl because they didn't know what to say; their ideas hadn't crystallised.

They were torn between wanting to be the good sports, the tolerant people, the liberals who took all that kind of thing casually, and, on the other side, the middle-aged couple to whom this girl's parents had given a daughter in the understanding that they would look after her. The words *in loco parentis* had been used in a letter. It literally meant in place of a parent.

So didn't they have a duty to know what the parents would have done under such circumstances, and then done something similar? They tried to read what the parents would have done. They voted Republican in the States which didn't give them any real indication. The father was a lawyer, the mother an interior decorator. It gave no hint of moral values and standpoint.

Years ago, when the London friend and the American friend had been together, of course they had got up to things. But they had been over 20 then. Not 17. But then, hadn't the world changed in those years? And anyway, weren't there always things that your parents were better off not knowing even if you were 50 and your parents 90?

As people unable to reach a decision, they did an intelligent thing. They left the house early next morning so as not to face the 17-year-old and the young man that she was either going to invite to breakfast or else bundle out the door. They asked their friends.

It's 1993. Were they mad to let her have this fellow in her room? Were they mad if they made a scene about it? They liked the girl, they could do with the rent. They didn't want to set the child adrift. They didn't want to have her staying with them fuming and mutinous. They didn't want to encourage adult, and possibly indiscriminate, relationships in a girl who might not be old enough to handle them. They didn't want to tell tales and have her shipped home.

There was no use in saying it was discourteous to bring an uninvited guest back to stay since everyone knew we weren't talking about courtesy, we were talking about sex. It was "asked-for advice".

I said she should ring the American friend immediately and say that, when they were making the checklist of things, like a glass of wine with dinner and what time she could travel on the Underground, she had forgotten to ask about having guys stay over. As if it hadn't happened yet. Then if she got an anguished squawk of "certainly not", she could pass this message on.

If she got a laid-back "what the hell; it's the end of the 20th century", she could think again and decide whether she wanted to go along with it or not. That way the *loco parentis* duty would have been fulfilled. If she were the 17-year-old's real mother, she'd have to make up her mind about things the way parents all over the world have to make up their minds, in the knowledge that whatever they do will be wrong.

But what she and her husband should not do is to lose another night's sleep over it. They must decide and act. There is probably no absolute right or wrong whatever they decide to do. In six months that girl will be old enough to make up her own mind.

They should ask for no more advice. What they were getting was an almost evenly divided "of course not" or "let them at it".

When you find yourself believing the last person you spoke to, you are in no position to make a decision. I think those of us who occasionally act in the place of real parents have as much right to make a mess of it as their own mothers and fathers do. But we have no right to dither and let them think, however accurately, that we don't know what we're doing.

SHADY DEALERS

*"How is he to know that society thinks what he does is wrong,
and that his fellow men and women do not believe it's good to
make money out of shady financial set-ups?"*

They rang up and asked would we come to supper next
week. They were having a few friends round to meet this
man . . . we didn't know him by any chance? No, but we
knew his name. He was in business in a big way and then
that business collapsed, owing a lot of money to people who
had invested in it. These weren't friends of his or
shareholders or gamblers who had taken a chance. They
were people who thought it was an ordinary place to put
their savings and now they had lost them.

The thing is that this man's lifestyle hasn't changed very
much, from what we hear.

I didn't want to go to a party to meet him, so I said I
wasn't free that night. Oh dear, what a huge statement of
moral principle there, you will say. There's real courage and
commitment in telling a social lie, right? But I didn't have
the arrogance – or what others might call courage – to say to
people, who had asked me to supper, that I disapproved of
their having invited such a man to their house. I don't have
the words to say a sentence about not wanting to share a
room or a meal with someone who, from all reports, thinks
little of having left other people's lives in ruin.

It's not because I am so fair-minded and generous that
I'm giving him the benefit of doubt or anything. In fact, I'm
almost certain he's a selfish go-getter who would open

another company in his wife's name without a backward glance, if he thought he could get away with it.

It's not that I'm afraid I would be unpopular if I were to say that it's wrong to treat people who cheat as half-heroes; to nod and wink and say wouldn't we all have done it, if we could.

But it's the gratuitous criticism that I would find hard to say. I would hate someone to tell me they wouldn't come to my house because they didn't like one of my friends. Similarly, if I were to discover later that someone had a deep-seated objection to another guest, then I would greatly prefer if they had made an excuse and not turned up. So I was doing as I would be done by.

Blameless, I thought.

Three other people I know were invited to the same party. One, a woman, found the vocabulary I couldn't find and said she couldn't possibly go because she so strongly disapproved of his behaviour. The second, a man, said he'd be delighted to go. When he meets the financier, he is going to ask him face to face how he can live with the fact that other people now have no reasonable living, due to him.

The third, a woman, said I had gone off my head. What right had I to pass judgement on other people? Did I operate a Back to Basics policy in relation to every guest, at every event, vetting them to know were they guilty of anything that offended a chic mode of behaviour before I agreed to join their number? She said, for all she knows, *half* the people she meets socially could beat their wives, falsify their tax returns, drive drunk and put the milk bottle on the table and yet she doesn't take pretentious decisions about whether or not she will admit them to her company.

"Would you seriously advise people not to go to a social

gathering where they know they are going to meet him?" she asked, eyes round in amazement.

Yes, I think I would.

I am *almost* certain.

She says I am being judgemental in the extreme. We have no idea what is going on in his mind; he could be giving money back to people secretly, hand over fist. Is he meant to go around wearing a hair shirt with a bell around his neck announcing his unclean arrival everywhere, so that he doesn't offend people like me who might accidentally be in the same room as him?

She said you wouldn't go out very often in Ireland if you were to check the credentials of everyone in the room. And perhaps there are people who mightn't like to meet *you*. Far better, she says, to keep an open mind about such things, meet everyone, smile at everyone. After all, you don't have to live with them or write them a reference.

But how is he to know that society thinks what he does is wrong, and that his fellow men and women do not believe it's good to make money out of shady financial set-ups? Does not the business of everyone accepting an invitation to meet him and smile at him not reinforce his feelings that his way of going on is perfectly acceptable?

I'm all for an easy life and, if I were to meet him casually somewhere, I think I would be civil, certainly in someone else's home. But I wouldn't *go* to meet him and I don't think it's despicable to pretend unavailability. I admire the courage of the man who said he would accept the invitation and then have a confrontation. But is it fair? On anyone? On the host? On the other guests? Even on the crooked financier, who may be under the impression that he had been invited for a pleasant night out?

I admire the courage of the woman who would state her reasons for not going, but she reminds me too much of another woman I know who says, accusingly, that I Speak As I Find. It has never really been a wise thing to do in terms of personal relationships.

And I'm not entirely sure that I admire myself in the middle of all this; mine is certainly the easiest option. But I have thought about it a lot. Suppose everyone had taken my advice. Suppose they had all said they weren't free that evening. Then the gathering would not be taking place.

Suppose they were all strong-minded enough not to go out and meet him but gentle enough not to damn by association the host who had invited them . . . then there would be no supper party. Life would go on, the crooked guy would see fewer smiling faces around him than, perhaps, he is used to seeing. I'm almost certain I'm right. The only trouble is that I keep getting a whiff of the Daughters of the American Revolution, with visions of social registers and people being blackballed if they are bankrupt. It would make you think of all those years when people were not allowed into the royal enclosure at Ascot if they were divorced until, suddenly, that included all the royals and the goal-posts were moved.

He's not in jail, he hasn't been prosecuted, he hasn't lost all his assets. I wouldn't lose any sleep if he lost a bit of social life and didn't find that everyone accepted that what he did was normal business behaviour.

Teetotal Tolerance

*"Publicans, who used to collapse like a Bateman cartoon
if anyone asked for coffee, now want to know if you
want decaf or cappuccino"*

A very agreeable, social sort of man, he says he won't come to Ireland for this particular gathering because he couldn't bear all the flak he will get about not taking a drink. He remembers Ireland in the old days, he says, when you brailled your way from the early Bloody Mary to the lunchtime pints and everyone was defined by the amount they could put away, while abstainers were mocked as Holy Joes, Cute Hoors or possibly Not Real Men.

Not the place for a man, four years into a different way of life, he says. Why draw it on himself? He's not afraid that he'll weaken or anything; it's just that he couldn't take all the explanations, the defensive attitude he will have to adopt, the rationalising, the assuring people that he doesn't object to *their* lifestyle, it's just that his own is not the same. He's been here before, he says; he knows of what he speaks. No, life is too short to take on that hassle. He's going to miss the reunion.

I advise him to think again and ask a few people, as well as myself, before he pleads an excuse not to meet classmates who were great pals in the years gone by. He may be very pleasantly surprised. The Ireland of his student days, 20 odd years ago, which he revisited 10 years ago, is not today's Ireland regarding attitudes to drink.

He will not find people calling him Matt Talbot or

Father Mathew if he asks for mineral water. They will not ask for an explanation, nor will they want one. And best of all, they will not turn red, watery eyes on him and sob into their own drinks about how they wished they had his strength. There are lots of nice pink livers in Ireland.

Ah, but Maeve was always one to see what she wanted to see, he says. I would like him to come and meet his fellow students so I could be expected to create a rose-tinted world for him where people are mature and wise and tolerant. This is not what he hears.

Right, I tell him, this is what I hear and see and notice. I notice that pubs, which love selling soft drinks anyway and always thrived on the mixers because they constitute almost pure profit, not attracting any tax, now have a whole rake of alcohol-free beers and low-alcohol lagers, and they are being wooed senseless by the various mineral-water manufacturers, dying to get their particular shade of bottle and label in.

Publicans, who used to collapse like a Bateman cartoon if anyone asked for coffee, now want to know if you want decaf or cappuccino. In recent years, I have not heard a barman make a joke about serving a Real Man a non-alcoholic drink. I haven't seen a sigh, or heard a groan. I have never heard an explanation about someone being a Pioneer, it being Lent, or the breathalyser, or the price of gargle being offered. Maybe I don't go to enough macho bars but I do go to a reasonable cross-section and in recent times I have never heard anyone being challenged after ordering the drink of his or her choice.

I agree that years ago the order would go, "Four pints, two gin-and-tonics, three large Paddies and a Cidona for your man!" Your man was thereby marked as being outside the tribe. Nowadays it's just as often the reverse; it could be a round of white wine and soda and many varieties of non or low-alcohol drinks and someone saying apologetically, "Do you mind if I have a short, it has been a bad day?"

Like smoking. People don't say they've given up apologetically. The apology is from the one who asks for the ashtray. I told the man who thinks that attitudes are frozen, that when I gave up smoking I was afraid to answer the telephone in case I had to have a cigarette before I spoke; I was unused to the experience of one without the other. Not a good example, he says. The phone wouldn't take me by the throat and say I was no fun without a cigarette – go on, have just one.

But I told him that he was guilty of over-dramatising himself. Everyone he will meet at his reunion will have read the bad news about how many units are safe per week. Some of them, admittedly, may have decided to take no notice, but they will *know* about them, they will not think he is wearing a hair-shirt and chains around his middle if he doesn't lower a bottle of sherry at the reception. Some of his colleagues and friends will have read the tests under the heading "Are you an alcoholic"? and by question three realised that they should be in treatment. Some will have done something, some will have said these questionnaires are run by some backlash pressure group. But they will have *read* them. There will be colleagues who have had friends die of drink-related illnesses, or passed over for promotion because of being a bit unreliable in that department.

He will discover that the liquid lunch is no longer a permanent feature of Irish middle-class life in the mainstream, as it might have been when he left. Not an eyebrow is raised if a captain of industry or a politician or even a successful journalist asks for a glass of water; heads will not wag. They will not say that's what has him where he is, either for good or evil. It's just one more choice people make. Like having no car and walking to work can be as high in the pecking order as having a car the size of a house. I advise him to give it a lash.

The profession that he is in has changed. Its ideas of machismo have altered greatly and not just because his colleagues have become middle-aged. New attitudes are all the more apparent among the younger generation. He may not find Ireland an entirely pluralist society but at least he will find his countrymen and women broad-minded enough to know that we owe no explanations for what forms of pleasure or madness we deny ourselves. And he will also have a great time.

SENSE AND CENSURE

"One day the mother or father will meet a sympathetic prelate or friend who will say something simple . . . but it will be too late"

Their only daughter was married in a far-off land last May. Neither of her parents was there. They couldn't attend a ceremony which was a sacrilege and a farce.

The man was already married. Well, he had gone through a form of "divorce" of course. His first marriage was over. "Over" was a word people used now when it suited them to say that a binding commitment was about to be abandoned for something marginally more interesting.

They had no personal hostility toward the man himself, but they will not allow you to call him their son-in-law.

They had actually liked him when their daughter had brought him home, when they hadn't realised that he was already a married man.

They would never accuse him of having seduced their daughter, or having made false promises. She had known from the very outset what the situation was and had gone along willingly. Don't get them wrong: they weren't casting him as a villain and her as a helpless wronged woman.

But it's the principle of the thing.

You have to have principles and stick to them; it's easy to shake your head and wag your finger at the deterioration of standards in other people and in other places. The crunch comes when it's in your own life. They are being tested, like the early Christians were tested – worship the Emperor and your life will be spared, say that you believe in the One True God and you will be thrown to the lions.

They had to stand up for what they believed was right. They had to tell her that it was no marriage and they couldn't lend it credibility and authority by attending it, by regarding it as anything except what it was.

Now they'd like you to know that it would have been much easier to have gone. *Much*. It wasn't a question of being afraid of what the neighbours would say, or what the priests in the parish would think. This was no stance taken for fear of public opinion. They are in their 50s; they don't consider themselves religious maniacs.

They just think they have a duty to say – however hard it is to say it – that their daughter has broken the rules of their faith and they will not go along with it.

If they truly believe this, then why can't they *let* her break the rules? They are not their daughter's keepers.

They say: you wouldn't look aside if your child stole or

cheated or was a drunken driver.

But surely they couldn't compare any of these things with marrying a man she loved, according to her own conscience?

They could and did, because the same situation prevailed: their daughter was in Mortal Sin and in danger of going to Hell for eternity. If they were to pretend that nothing was amiss, they would be helping their daughter towards damnation.

They found it alarming that people should say that Hell was all gone now in the new teaching of the church. Where did people find this comforting view? They admitted that there had been some changes: the Latin Mass, the nature of guardian angels, the rules on fast and abstinence – and they were not against these changes. Please don't believe they were members of some Old Guard resisting every forward step.

But the whole purpose of being on earth was to work for Salvation, wasn't it? And no one ever said it was going to be easy.

And it's not Victorian, you know. It's not as if they don't mention her name, or refuse to acknowledge that she exists. They sent her a letter at Christmas and she sent them one. She also wrote in the New Year and said she was expecting a child in the summer. They haven't replied to that letter yet.

Now *of course* they're not going to take it out on an innocent child. The danger of having any kind of standards is that people will paint you as unfeeling ogres. They don't have stereotyped bigoted beliefs that the child will be illegitimate or anything. Such a word isn't in their vocabulary any more than it is in the law.

Yes, it would have been different if this man had his

marriage annulled. Of course it would. Then it would be a question of no previous marriage having existed. Then he would have been free to marry in a church and everything would have been all right.

But would they not agree that the man was being honourable in admitting that his first marriage of seven years *had* existed rather than finding a series of excuses and explanations to prove that it hadn't?

No, they could not agree with this, they would have to think that, since he knew his first marriage was a real one, he should also know that it was not capable of being dissolved.

I think I am presenting their view fairly. But I have met their daughter in a far-off land. A girl living miles from home because she could not bear the tension and stress that living near her parents would involve.

She lives in a big housing estate in a sprawling suburb of a city that she hasn't really come to know and make her own. Her husband has a job with long hours, meaning he is away from home a good deal more than either of them would like.

She has two jobs, one in a flower shop in the mornings, and in the afternoons she types theses and manuscripts on a word processor. Her mother does not know about either of these jobs – the letters she wrote home were deliberately short and spare on detail. Her parents had told her that they could not pretend to assume a delight and interest in her everyday life when she knew how grievously they disapproved of the whole situation.

She is desperately lonely. She plays Irish music all the time. She made a journey of two buses and a train to attend an Irish book signing. Her neighbours who are having children have letters of encouragement from home. There are future grannies and grandfathers saving the fare to come out and see infants and toddlers. A group of her friends have bought a video camera to share so that they can send pictures home. She joins in because it would look so strange not to – but she will have no one to send the video cassette to. Yes, she does have friends back in Ireland; but it would seem somehow even sadder to send one to them and not to her home.

You don't have to be super-intelligent to know that it will all be made up some day. But when? When the parents are in their late 70s? 80s? When they are old and sad at the lost years, the lack of a daughter and grandchildren?

One day the mother or father will meet a sympathetic prelate or friend who will say something simple: if there is a God then a God would not want a parent to cut off a child because of a principle.

But it will be too late. A lifetime of memories and reunions and love will have been allowed to slip away. They will take their dog for a walk and wish they had grandchildren to push along the pier on a Sunday when they came home for a visit. She will play more and more Irish tunes and make her homeland into a fantasy island. He will work longer and harder hours to buy her the things he hopes will make her happy.

And all the time a principle will have been honoured by two good people who truly believed that this was the time of their testing.

Speedy Dispatch

*"That's something we should remove from the national
psyche . . . the notion that a letter might be an intrusion"*

A woman said to me the other day that she had voted
Labour all her life until the last election, when she literally
couldn't give a vote to either candidate in Dublin because
she was so utterly fed up with the campaign antics and the
in-fighting. She also feared that Labour was sort of turning
into Fianna Fáil. So she voted for the little Green girl, as she
called her. But she didn't feel good about it.

Nobody would ever know what had changed a loyalty
that she would have once thought of as unswerving. The
party would see its vote down and not really know what had
been in individual hearts and minds when it came to voting
time. What a pity, she said, that we can't put down our
reasons for voting for or against a party, or candidate, on the
back of the ballot paper.

Well, for the price of a stamp, she could express her
views. She hadn't thought of writing letters to them, she
said – politicians don't want to hear long, hectoring tirades
from people out there, especially people who didn't vote for
them?

That may be true, but such a letter doesn't have to be
long or hectoring or even a tirade. Politicians, if they are in
touch with reality, should want to hear a brief, reasoned
explanation as to why they have lost your support. Even if
they think you are barking. And suppose 10,000 people
wrote to Dick Spring and said that these were their views?

Then he would have to take it on board. And suppose 10,000 people who once had Fianna Fáil blood coursing through their veins wrote to Albert Reynolds and said that they really felt the business of granting passports didn't have a kosher explanation and, even though he may well be as pure as the driven snow, it had produced an aura of Banana Republicanism about it that was unsuited to the Soldiers of Destiny – well, then Albert would know that a lot of people out there were uneasy and cynical.

And suppose 10,000 people wrote to Mary Harney saying that they could no longer believe that the PDs had any new philosophy because all they seemed to do was shoot themselves, and each other, in the foot. And then 10,000 people could write to John Bruton saying that since the Tallaght Strategy had been let go, it was very hard to know what Fine Gael was *for* – only what it was against.

These are the kinds of things people say in conversation. They don't meet the people who could do anything about them, all they can do is vote for them and the woman is absolutely right to feel frustrated. How will the politicians ever know the real reasons for discontent, disappointment and the eventual falling off of support unless we tell them?

Of course they can read the papers and watch the television analysis and listen to the radio programmes. But these are the views of radio commentators, chat show hosts, newspaper columnists. On vox pop or access programmes, these are the voices of the committed, the politically active, the extroverted, and often the notice boxes who want to have their say and be heard saying it. The so-called Ordinary People, whose support politicians are trying to get, are often a mystery, since their considered view is not adequately expressed.

They are wooed with promises of a better life, of lower taxes, of more jobs and ever-bigger hauls from the bottomless pits of Europe. There isn't time in the sound-bite system to talk about idealism and hopes and dreams of what this country might be like. The speeches are a one-way business. They tell us what they think we want to hear. If we haven't told them what we want them to do, then is it fair to expect them to know?

Most of us have some sort of idea of how we would like the country to be run, and one of the parties must come nearest to that hope. So why don't we write and tell that party truthfully what we think it could do?

The woman who won't write to Dick Spring dismissed this argument. He would just think it was from a crank, a nutter; he would move on through the letter wanting to know what particular favour she wanted. He would think she was a professional letter-writer, a person with time on her hands and an outsize ego. Why bother? It would be put in the wastepaper basket, or else answered courteously, in a meaningless, time-consuming way, by someone who dealt with these things.

But my point is this. If he got thousands of these letters, they could not be ignored. By nature, we are not a shrugging, cynical race which has abandoned the running of things to the cowboys. We have always been able to express our views and this is what makes us more interesting and volatile than many another race. But I think we have forgotten the art of the letter, as the old-fashioned manuals used to call it, and we have forgotten the power of many, many letters.

We are bad at writing thank you notes, cards of congratulations and even fan letters. We think they won't want to be bothered hearing all that. This is madness. People love to be praised, they love it to bits, we all love it to bits.

So that's something we should remove from the national psyche . . . the notion that a letter might be an intrusion.

And, if something has gone disastrously wrong, if we have stopped voting for the party we always supported, I think it's courteous, practical, reasonable and helpful to write a letter explaining why. That way they won't have to interpret the polls, the pundits and the rumour factory. That way they will actually know, from people with the courage to include their name and address, and the restraint to keep their tone civilised and positive.

The woman who wished she could express her views on her ballot paper was underselling herself. There wouldn't be room. She would need at least one side of a sheet of paper and we should write the letters now.

Naming the Criminal

"Rape is a crime and must be considered one. To ignore it and just cross the street when she sees this man again is to diminish, even in his eyes, what he did"

She is 20 and she doesn't know me, but I know a great friend of her mother's. She was at a party three weeks ago, and she went there with this fellow. He wasn't her boyfriend, but he was a friend.

There was a lot of messing about, quite a bit of drink, but she was definitely not drunk. People began to drift into different rooms. She was disappointed that the party seemed to be falling to pieces, but her friend seemed very pleased. He pulled her onto a sofa and raped her.

Nobody heard her shouting for help because there was loud music. She had been dancing with him earlier but she swears she had not encouraged him in any way. They hadn't even kissed each other, for God's sake. He was much bigger and stronger than she was. He told her throughout that she was dying for it.

She got away from the party and came home. She couldn't sleep. She was frightened and hurt. And she also felt that it was her own fault.

When her mother found her the next morning, still sitting beside her window and in great distress, she reluctantly told her what had happened.

Her mother was hugely sympathetic and supportive. She gave all the hugging and moral encouragement she could. Not a word of blame, or regret that she had gone to such a party.

And then when the girl said she was going to tell the guards, her mother's face froze.

"You can't possibly do that," she said in astonishment. "This has nothing to do with the guards, it wasn't a stranger that came and raped you, it was a boy you went out with. You knew what you were doing when you went to the party with him. Nobody would call that rape, they'll say it was a normal and even reasonable end to the evening."

Now the mother doesn't think it *was* a normal, reasonable end to the evening, but she thinks that's what the authorities will say. It's like calling the guards to a fight between husband and wife . . . they'll have to say, regretfully, that it's a domestic matter. And if it gets to the courts? Well then, surely, there will be all kinds of questioning and investigating and does she really want to explain the night's activities, in detail, in open court, to people who will all assume that it was a matter of consent anyway?

"You mean he's going to get away with it? Isn't it a crime?" the girl asked.

"You don't have to see him again, and the trauma of the whole thing would be as bad as the rape," said her mother, who was utterly sincere and had no hidden agenda about fear of publicity or scandal or anything like that.

And this week, with all the publicity about the case in England where the King's College student, Austin Donnellan, refused to submit to a college disciplinary punishment and insisted that, if he had to be charged with rape, then he should be tried in open court, has seemed very relevant to them.

In the Old Bailey in London, Austin Donnellan was entirely cleared of rape because it was decided that the girl was drunk and willing. Hate mail has gathered in sackfuls against the girl who had wrongly accused the male student who was brave enough to give his name, even though hers has been kept a secret. It seemed to prove what a lot of people suspected, that women were quite enthusiastic and then regretted it and then cried rape.

The mother and daughter read the reports and were glad they had not filed a complaint on the friend who had taken her to the party – even though he had proved to be such a false friend.

If it had been a stranger . . . now, that would have been totally different, they told each other. Then she would have been blameless. No one could have said it was all her fault.

If it were defined as rape at all, it would be called "date rape", with all the complicity that that term implies.

That is not a phrase that should be used.

We don't talk about dating as part of our normal conversation in this country. You say someone is going out with someone on Friday, not dating them, or that people are seeing each other, not dating each other. Why choose this phrase to cover such a hugely controversial and important aspect of rape? The expression "date rape" minimises rape. It is also misleading – 80 per cent of the rapes committed in Ireland are by people known to the victim.

In cases of "stranger rape" – to use another made-up expression – women are much more likely to report it. It's not as hard to describe violation by a totally unknown person, and there isn't the lurking fear that it might be seen to have been condoned or encouraged.

Of those who consult the Rape Crisis Centre in Dublin, only 30 per cent will go to the guards and, of that number, only 10 per cent will go to court. The centre agrees with this mother and daughter's view, that rape by a stranger is somehow more socially acceptable, if you could use such a phrase in this context.

Some of the girl's friends are encouraging her to bring charges against him. If he had assaulted her in some other way, she would; if he had robbed her, she would have no hesitation. She was hesitating because she feared that the intimacy he forced upon her would be regarded as part of something agreed between them.

Some of her friends have said that statistics have shown that someone who rapes is likely to rape again. All right, so she might not see him again, but what about all the other women he is likely to meet in his life? Does she not owe them any responsibility?

Her mother has heard that going to court is a nightmare.

The victim is not legally represented, she appears only as witness for the State. There are proposals to change that, but this is the way it stands at the moment. The girl can look at a group of wigs and not know which one is for her and which one is against.

If she doesn't accuse him of rape, she may forget it more easily.

Or, if she does accuse him, perhaps she will have somehow exorcised it and played a part in establishing that rape is a crime and must be considered one. To ignore it and just cross the street when she sees this man again is to diminish, even in his eyes, what he did.

She doesn't hate men, nor does she want them branded as beasts. She is torn between the beliefs that it is best forgotten or best tackled.

I'd advise her to tell.

Too many people have not told things over the years because it was going to cause more trouble, or get too involved, or cause more heartbreak, than it was worth. Often they think that to report a crime such as rape would be a sort of act of revenge, and therefore almost as tainted as the original offence.

Always, in the case of reporting someone you know, there is a huge conflict of interests. But if she were to ask the people who know, the people who work for the Rape Crisis Centre, she would hear words and statistics that would give her courage. The courage to know that sleeping dogs – if they are rapists – should not be allowed to lie.

YOUNG NICKS

*"If parents gloat over not paying VAT on something,
shouldn't a child try to escape the fare on the DART?"*

They were in the carpark, unpacking the trolley from the
supermarket. Her nine-year-old son was being very helpful as
usual and, as he went to return the trolley to the queue, she
saw him pausing to open a Kit Kat.

"Hey, where did you get that?" she asked.

He reddened and said nothing.

"Did you steal it?" she asked. There was no reply.

"You can't take things without paying for them."

"I'm sorry," he said, with his head down.

The mother said it was a very long moment. She didn't
want to force him to go back with it and say he had stolen
it. She didn't want to say anything about how shaming it
would be if he had been caught, because that made the
being caught bit worse than the actual act of taking it.

But she thought, come on, he's only a kid. Kids like Kit
Kats. Supermarkets leave them where kids can see them, to
drive them mad with desire for them. Supermarkets build in
the cost of kids nicking things. It's not a federal crime. She
should lighten up and let it go. Otherwise, when it comes to
really heavy things where she wants to lay down the law –
like about drugs and motor-bikes – she won't have any
authority. He'll always think of her as a nit-picking mother,
who thinks that the most minimal things are major deals.

So after what seemed like a lot of thought, she said: "All
right this time, but don't do it again, you get pocket money

and that's what it's for". And he cheered up, finished the bar, and got into the car companionably beside her.

For him, the incident was over. For his mother, it was not. "Did I do the right thing?" she asked. A lot of people said yes.

They said that supermarkets were almost open season. They said that big companies like that expected to lose the odd bar here and there and wouldn't even know how to ring through an empty wrapper paper if it were returned by a humiliated nine-year-old and his gaoler mother.

They said there was stealing and *stealing*. A child swiping a chocolate bar from a supermarket shelf wasn't the real thing. Now, if he had taken one from another child, it really *would* have been stealing. Then she would have something to worry about. It showed a totally different sort of nature if a kid stole from another kid's schoolbag or coat pocket. But from a shelf of them? No.

And then there were those who said that maybe it was a sign that something was wrong. She shouldn't look on it as a simple act of shoplifting, but as an indication that the boy wasn't getting enough love or attention at home. She thought about that seriously and decided that, as a theory, it didn't hold any water.

Theirs was a happy home. There had been no new arrival to wipe his eye, no latchkey child syndrome, no absent father, no rows, no fear that the marriage wasn't stable. In all honesty she couldn't see that it was a cry for help. Just a cry for a Kit Kat. And a refusal to spend his pocket money on it.

And other reassuring friends said: "It wasn't as if it was money. Don't worry if they only take small things, that's natural. Now money from someone's handbag, that would be different".

But she asks herself, suppose it *is* a handbag next time?

If he thinks she'll keep an eye on him in supermarkets from now on, might he not help himself to the coins from her bag? Or, a thousand times worse, from someone else's handbag? And why would it be worse from someone else's bag? The amount would be the same, the action would be the same.

She realised that it's the shame element that would make one theft greater than the other. What kind of morality was that?

I'd advise that she should have gone back with the Kit Kat. Not with a heavy moral tone and drumbeats of doom, but quite casually, saying: "Look, we forgot to pay for this, sorry . . . Can we pay for it now?" Then the point would have been made.

There couldn't be *à la carte* nicking, some of which was tolerated and some of which wasn't.

Children are very logical. Why, if the odd bar of chocolate is okay, wouldn't the odd bottle of sherry be fine for the adult to take? If parents gloat over not paying VAT on something, shouldn't a child try to escape the fare on the DART?

People will say that times have changed since my youth, when a girl of 12 was reported to the school for having stolen a packet of clear gums from a station stall. And we thought she was terrible. Nowadays, kids go into shops and hoover up what's available, they tell you.

But that's not what anyone would call the march of progress or the dawn of a new enlightenment. And it is not the way parents should view it. Of course it's easier when you have no children, things are more absolute, the areas less grey. But even those with no children love them and want the best for them. If I were with a nine-year-old, I'd go back to the till with a cheery face and no post-mortems over a nicked bar of chocolate.

You can't expect children to look into your face and wonder is this kind of theft acceptable – or not – unless there are some guidelines, however old-fashioned, laid down, for them.

CASTE STRUGGLE

"A sense of tribal mistrust will never be solved by a new batch of statistics, however accurate and however damning to the racist war of words"

It was a long way to the reading at the Writers and Readers Festival in Birmingham. We passed two mosques, endless rows of shops selling saris, very sweet sugary confectionery, stores with bags of flour to make chapati-type bread. The children playing in the school-yards were of all colours. The signs over shops and business premises were in foreign lettering. It would not take a fleet of detectives to work out that Birmingham is a multinational city.

The remarks of Tory MP Winston Churchill – who, because of his name, would get media attention if he only read the telephone book – hit Birmingham hard. He spoke of a "relentless flow" of immigrants into the country and of "our northern cities being over 50 per cent immigrant". He called for a halt to immigration, and said that the face of Britain was changing in ways that did not have the consent of its people.

Like Enoch Powell's famous "rivers of blood" speech all those years ago, his words provoked both alarm and fear.

They had to be taken back, of course, explained, and elaborated. He wrote to *The Times*: "When I spoke about our northern cities being 50 per cent immigrant, I only meant the *inner* cities". This, when his figures were immediately challenged.

The British Home Office had to come out and pat people down by assuring them that only the families and dependants of British subjects were being allowed to immigrate, and denied that it was a "relentless flow". So it meant that everyone was apologising for the existence of Asians in the country and trying to say there weren't nearly as many there, nor on the way, as Winston Churchill had said.

And then began the pub talk. A latter-day Alf Garnett said that maybe the man had a point. Why shouldn't such things be discussed? This wasn't what they had fought two World Wars for.

It couldn't have come at a worse time for Mary. It coincided with the week she had decided to tell her parents that she would marry Jalid. They know about him, of course, they've met him and have been polite – on the whole. When her father has had a few pints on a Sunday, he sometimes asks how it is that Mary couldn't find one of her own kind to take up with. But Mary says that this kind of thing goes with the territory of Sunday lunch at your parents' house. Something is *always* a mystery to parents – the length of skirts, of hair, of time on the phone, in the bathroom, or not in the bathroom. It was only to be expected that finding love in another community would be a mystery as well.

Mary is a teacher and lives in her own flat. When it became serious with Jalid, she did her best to prepare for arguments by involving her mother in the school so that she could meet little Pakistani children at first hand and not fear the possibility of being a grandmother to an alien kind.

Jalid's mother doesn't speak English and Mary has enough problems trying to work out what the small, anxious foreign woman thinks of her to even contemplate bringing the two families together in any farcical pretence of bonhomie. She and Jalid have decided that the wedding will involve a lot of hand-shaking introductions, and then two distinct groups at either end of a function room. They could survive it, they told each other, up to the new war of words. Now everything has changed.

The older generation in Jalid's family has bought very strong shutters for the windows of the small shops that they run. His father has urged him seriously not to be seen holding Mary's hand in public, in case it might inflame a gang of skinheads.

Mary's father said that, if she could get a career break, he would be happy to give her a few quid to get out of Birmingham and see a bit more of the world. All right, so he did say there was no place like home, once. But that was a while ago and a person could be wrong, couldn't they? Mary's mother has spoken not once, but twice, about the marriage bureau at Knock.

Mary is so stung by the injustice of it all that she is not thinking practically any more; she is thinking in statistics which will not change any mind or heart that she wants to change. She will point to surveys, independent surveys, not ones undertaken with a bias. Immigrants from India, Pakistan and Bangladesh, she will prove to you, are far higher in what are defined as the acceptable values that British society desires.

Even the census shows that, in 80 per cent of Asian

families, there are two parents and children, so how could anyone say that they are battening off the State? Milking the welfare services? You only had to look at their record in looking after the elderly in their extended families: they didn't *need* paid welfare visitors or places in old people's homes.

Mary says she can't understand why people turn away from these statistics; if you read them, it's as plain as the nose on your face, that the Asian community is no threat, no drain on the country's resources. Why can't there be a proper campaign to counteract this whisper war from the Winston Churchill faction which claims that the number of immigrants each year is in excess of the whole population of Grantham? Things will not change, Mary cries, until everyone is told the facts.

I don't agree. I think Mary should forget the facts and concentrate on people and life-stories. She should bring Jalid around to her parents for his breakfast, dinner and tea, if she wants them to understand him. She should encourage him to tell her father all about the place where he works (making the new Pullman cars for the Channel Tunnel trains), and all the luxuries they will have – videos, maplewood desks, telephones in each room. She should forget charts about the stability of Asian family life and quibbles over numbers let in at Heathrow. She should include his nephews and nieces with their Brummie accents. She should talk about the members of his family whom she loves, and whisper about the ones she dislikes, just as she would do if they were *not* from Pakistan.

She should bring up, good-naturedly, all the fuss there was in the 1950s when her own parents married across the cultural divide, at a time when "No Irish" was written in landladies' windows, and when her mother's people thought that marrying an Englishman was the greatest sell-out since the marriage of Aoife to Strongbow.

A sense of tribal mistrust will never be solved by a new batch of statistics, however accurate and however damning to the racist war of words. The weapons that the thousands of Jalids and Marys must use have got everything to do with wearing down prejudice by sheer familiarity, and nothing at all to do with an intellectual appeal. The host community will not read the evidence and accept that it is not being swamped by newcomers.

What Mary should bring to Sunday lunch tomorrow is Jalid – and not the study from Warwick University proving what a splendid and non-intrusive role Jalid's tribe is playing in the area.

Her Irish mother and English father will never learn to love statistics. But they might well accept as normal and, eventually even as good, a marriage where a man and woman refuse even to dignify the problems by defining and denying them.

FIRST COMPROMISE

"It's not blackmail, it's not super indulgence, it's knowing that you can't change the world between now and Corpus Christi"

All right, the young mother says, all right, she knows the arguments, you can't disappoint a child. It is not the little girl's fault that the country has become obsessed with show and competition and vulgar display. But *someone* has to make a stand. Either it's a religious milestone, and an important part of a person's spiritual life – if so then of course it should be marked and honoured – or it's not. And, for the great majority of those entering into the Communion and Confirmation circuses this month, there is little spirituality. When she hears of seven-year-old girls applying fake tan to their little legs to look well in the photographs, that annoys her marginally less than their mothers going to the Canaries to get real tans to look dazzling in the church in pale pink jackets and low-cut blouses.

This woman is 33 and she has a daughter and a son. She has a husband who was recently made redundant. She has a job where she works long hours. They have a house which could be a lot more comfortable if there were two salaries coming in. They have friends, neighbours and family around. She is not a loner. She is head of no cause. She never stood on a principle against the crowd, before this. She is not doing it for God. She thinks that God is indulgent and forgiving about the way humans make such a mess out of everything including what is meant to be a sacrament.

No, she wants to stand alone against the charade because she thinks it's dangerous for little girls to be made into princesses for a day with everyone admiring their dress, their ringlets, their flowers, the professional taker of photographs, the video of a big lunch party with a host of relatives and friends fielded.

Because it's the first step on a ladder. Then there will be the Confirmation, and the Debs and the Engagement and the Wedding and the Christening. She says she can't listen any more to those who say that life is grey enough, and that it's colourful and good to mark out the happenings along the way with pageantry.

In her job she has come across the seriously poor. Her everyday work involves trying to put together the pieces for people deep in a well of poverty in a world of moneylenders. It is only too obvious to see that the spiral begins with the loans for the First Communion outfit.

She can date almost every loan pattern to the time when the eldest child was seven. She says that, up to now, she went along with the indulgent view that life had to have its compensations, that it was not fair to deny those who had so little, their days of dressing up and being able to stand heads high watching a little princess come out of the church rather than a kid in the clothes, the unsatisfactory clothes, of every day.

Now she thinks this view is patronising. It smacks of allowing the poor to have processions and pageants and to pretend to be the rich for one day a year. She sees what the expectations of a middle-class child are going to cost, and she feels it personally. They will not put themselves into debt over this. She will *not* approach her credit union for a loan even though she is luckier than those who have to go out and borrow from moneylenders.

Scales have fallen from her eyes, she says. She sees the other mothers, not as wonderful, kind, maternal creatures doing their best for a child's big day, but as ludicrous, competitive entrants in a surreal Miss World contest. They are living out their own fantasies in the dresses, the curls, the flowers and the photographs. They are grumbling because camcorders are not allowed into the church; they are saying that kill-joys are trying to spoil it for the youngsters. Trying to be all sour and take away their big day.

And she believes with all her heart that a seven-year-old child will be happy with any kind of fuss . . . not just this out-of-control commercial fuss. All it needs is for someone to have the courage to opt out, to give the child a great day without the razzmatazz.

She was disappointed that I didn't agree. She would have thought I wouldn't want to go for all this show, that I'd like it to be like the old days. It's no use thinking about the past, what it was like in the old days.

I have my First Communion picture like everyone has. I look like a happy lampshade, there was something odd about the wreath. We went to see my aunt in the convent; it was just after the war and the trams and buses were so slow it took all day, but I didn't mind. I had people admiring me for hours.

I don't remember my Confirmation day, although I have a picture of myself in school uniform but wearing a plain net veil. The nuns, very admirably, urged families not to spend a great deal of money on outfits, which was sensible, but they didn't give us a big party in the school, which was foolish. We felt like anyone else. My face has all the lines of being short-changed.

I think this mother *should* borrow the money and give her daughter the day. Her husband is very supportive; he says he would love his little girl to look and feel the equal of everyone else at her school. He doesn't see it as a principle. And that is what their real difference is all about.

I do see it as a principle. But, because she's much, much too late, she has missed the principle bus. And she has to give in, this time anyway. It really is not fair that a seven-year-old should be made the victim of her stance. It's all very well to say that a seven-year-old heart doesn't break seriously and the child will cheer up again, but it's not honest. It's not only the day itself. It is the weeks afterwards when they are all still talking about it and showing the pictures. How can a girl that age explain what her mother finds difficult to put into words, even if she were to understand it?

There are many more years of misconstruing for her mother ahead, many rows to be fought, chasms to be opened between them, words to be said and taken back, plea bargains to be arranged. Let her not have the additional weapon and aching hurt that at seven, when every single other child had a day like a princess, Mother took a silly stand and wouldn't let the child do it.

It's not blackmail, it's not super indulgence, it's knowing that you can't change the world between now and Corpus Christi.

The little lad is only four. She has three years to work on his school, to try to get it turned into a school day where all the parents can come and contribute food and give money to a good cause. There can be group pictures and family snaps. The notion of collecting money can be frowned upon.

Most mothers are misunderstood much of the time. Let her not go for it like a lemming by depriving her daughter of a day that was hers by right of having *expected* it.

TREADING ON DREAMS

"Of course it's a dream. We can't buy certain happiness"

This summer over 30,000 people will leave Ireland for Florida alone, many of them on family holidays. For two grown-ups and two children it can cost £1,300 for two weeks. That will include the fares, an apartment and a hired car. They pay for petrol and food and drink the same as they would at home.

This family has been saving since Christmas and they'll be heading off in about three weeks' time. Their neighbours shake their heads and say they are quite mad.

First, they say these are not wealthy people. They have very ordinary jobs, the mother and father. The house could do with a coat of paint, the children don't have clothes or shoes that are up to standard. They don't have a lawnmower and, in the summer, their garden has a straggly look about it.

This couple have a cheap and smelly oil heater in their hall, the kind of thing that you wouldn't feel safe with at all. They might be better getting some kind of heating, cleaning up their act a bit, instead of filling two children's heads with nonsense out in Florida, no less.

These are not just jealous, selfish neighbours, nor killjoys who are against the lower orders having a holiday as if they were people of property. They are not the house-proud, neighbourhood-conscious folk who would want to confiscate the air tickets and replace them with two cans of paint and a strimmer to keep up standards.

The neighbours really and truly think that the whole business of getting passports and visas, and studying maps of the east coast of the US, is only laying up a store of unhappiness in the long run. The word they use is *unrealistic*. They say it's *unrealistic* for people, who live at the level that they do, to raise the expectations of the children who are, after all, only 12 and 10 and would be content with something a quarter the cost, and much nearer home.

I don't think it's ridiculous. I think it's about the most realistic thing they could do. They have been earning around £45 extra a week between them, and the children have been encouraged to do baby-sitting in order to have some pocket-money to spend when they get there.

If you are going to work in a supermarket, sweep up in a hairdressing salon on late nights, do deliveries, or a couple of nights washing up in a restaurant, then surely the best thing is to have a nice near goal that you can actually see ahead of you.

I would prefer to work for a ticket from Shannon to Miami and to look at the picture of the car I was going to rent, the apartment where we would all stay, to imagine the faces of children brought to Disney World in Orlando, than to think in some vague terms of improvement of lifestyle. I don't go along with the theory that because saving for a holiday is, in fact, buying a dream, we shouldn't do it.

Of course it's a dream. We can't buy certain happiness. That family will probably find the heat too much, the children may be difficult and not grateful enough, or delighted enough, the apartment might well be too small, or too remote. They might meet nobody from home and be lonely, they might meet everyone from home and feel crowded out; they might, on the other hand, have a ball. But whatever happens, they will have gone to a different place, a place miles from here, and they will have been able to show that kind of a place to their children.

Why should that privilege belong only to those who were born to it, or those who had worked for so many decades to earn it that they were too feeble to enjoy it once they felt they had saved enough to go there?

There is, still, a snobbish begrudging attitude that the needy shouldn't have a holiday – an idea which holds no water at all, since the lowest brain must accept that they should have one much sooner than those whose everyday life is full of treats and variety. But you would not have to dig deep to find the view that, if people knew their place, they should realise that this place was not as a part of a foreign holiday.

The argument went on long about this family. I was accused of being a reverse snob, my attitude equally patronising, if not more so. I was just patting them on the head, I was told. I was encouraging them to go on and take a holiday that was out of step with their economic circumstances because I wanted to appease my own conscience and feel good that others too had trips abroad.

It became fairly heated, which is not necessarily bad. But it may be one of those insoluble things, like those who are cold not being able to understand those who are hot. The neighbours, the people who say this family is just increasing its downwards economic spiral, can see nothing but waste in handing over £1,300 to a travel agency.

They remind me that I was fiercely intolerant of the people who threw away their money in Las Vegas. I remember my attitude there as being mature, wise, tolerant but mystified. Still, I take the argument and run with it. In gambling you risk losing all you worked for. In spending it on a two-week blast, you have made a choice of how you are going to spend it. If you want to sit under the sun and drink strange, coloured drinks, like lots of us do, then why, if you are not cheating anyone else, should you not do so?

This is the same as my encouraging people to waste money on Communion frocks, they said. No it's not. It's different. That's so that a child won't feel left out of a cultural scene. Not even on my most giddy highs could I think that it's part of the norm to go to Florida, and that those two children will be scarred if they don't get there.

It would be indeed patronising and reverse snobbery to pretend that I was ever very poor but I didn't have much to spend as a young teacher. I think it's fair to say that there wasn't anything sizeable. And of *course* I should have bought a good winter coat and leather shoes but I didn't; I saw the world.

There were many of my parents' friends who would have liked them to buy a car, or go out to restaurants for a meal, or put in central heating. But my parents didn't want what people said were sensible things. What was left over from educating the lot of us, they spent on taking us on a holiday every year. It wasn't Fort Lauderdale by plane, it was Ballybunion by train – but for seven of us, for a month, that was pricy too. And in terms of memory and widening of horizons and seeing another world, it was worth every penny.

Some time in the middle of the next millennium those children whose house is a mess, whose garden is a wilderness and whose parents are needy will remember the holiday in Florida. Surely it's not patronising to wish them well?

MISTER WRONG

"Nobody else has had the guts to say anything except squeak about how romantic it is . . ."

Sometime soon, within the next few months, this couple will get married. That's the plan anyway. I am not on the guest list of 60 people, and I only know the bride very indirectly. But I do know that at least four of the people who will attend the wedding think very strongly that she should not be getting married at all.

I don't know anyone on the groom's side, so we have no

reading from his side of the church. Four people who know her well, is this a very sizeable amount of opposition? Or is it the norm?

For all we know. Maybe weddings are filled with people dressed to kill and *fuming* inside about the union that is taking place in front of their eyes. Maybe most people believe most marriages are unwise and forecast doom under their breath as they cheerfully throw handfuls of confetti.

And, of course, most people shut up about it. The words just don't exist to tell someone that you think they have made a poor choice of a life-mate.

If, in return for your wedding invitation, you handed out a great chunk of Unasked-for Advice, and pointed out the weak links in the chain, the glaring incompatibilities and the wisdom of celibacy at this point, you would find yourself fairly friendless.

But suppose, just suppose for a moment that you were right. Suppose that you could see why these two people might be making a mistake, spurred on by all the pressures of society and a series of shallow attitudes. Suppose you truly believed it. Should you say anything, or should you forever hold your peace?

One of the wedding guests is on the verge of doing the unthinkable and actually saying what others are thinking. She thinks that this girl is marrying because she is 30, because she feels it's her last chance. Because all her friends are married and she feels out of it.

She believes that, in spite of the giant steps made in giving self-confidence to women, many of them still feel that their place is, if not in the kitchen, at least marching two-by-two with a male of the species to shopping malls on a Saturday, to garden centres on a Sunday, and through all the paraphernalia that being married brings in its wake.

But surely an intelligent girl in the 1990s wouldn't marry just to say she was married, rather than because she had met a real person to share her life with properly?

Ah, says the Courageous Wedding Guest, there's another side of this. There's the aspect of loneliness. It's hard to see everyone else sharing, and having someone to talk to, if you don't have it yourself. When she comes home from work, there's nobody to tell about the horrors of the day. At breakfast, there's no one to tell her she looks well or has a run in her tights or to make plans with.

But, if this is the problem, why doesn't she look for a flatmate? Or a lodger? Or indeed a lover? Marriage seems a bit drastic a solution to ease a small sense of isolation, or a need-more-conversation phase. No, there's something makeshift and temporary about such arrangements. And anyway, the bride-to-be has looked around her. If everyone else on Planet Earth has found a spouse, so can she. It's as simple and as deeply unsatisfactory as that.

All right, let's suppose that her frame of mind has been correctly analysed. Lots of people marry unlikely-seeming people. What's so wrong with this one that people seem to be going into conclave over him?

The answer was that he was, basically, a very stupid man. Something that the faint-hearted would find hard to speak aloud as a reason for his betrothed to renounce him at this late stage. But that is what he was.

He read nothing except magazines concerned with a hobby. He looked at sport on television but didn't like any current affairs programmes or films. He shrugged at politics. "They're all the same, they're in it for what they can get."

I asked whether everyone else's objections were based on

a similar set of premises – basically that she was too bright for this guy. Well, yes and no. The man was a bit restless. He had been in a relationship for three years and *that* had not worked out. He had changed jobs often. He never kept a car for a full year.

Someone has to play the Devil's Advocate . . . These could be *good* signs, I argued. He knew the last relationship wasn't right so they hadn't married. He's not stuck in a rut as regards work. Maybe the car thing has something to do with tax?

He had nothing to say to her friends, she seemed constantly defensive about him . . . she moved the conversation from topics that bored him to things that the tabloid newspapers might have on page one.

The Courageous Wedding Guest was, I believe, a really good and honourable friend. She didn't live in the same town as the bride-to-be. It wasn't a simple matter of jealousy, the sense of loss we all feel when a friend gets married and isn't available as much as before. I may have made her sound a total snob and an elitist, but it was very hard for her to articulate those criticisms; they weren't dismissive, middle-class attitudes that would trip easily off a class-ridden tongue.

She is not a killjoy by nature, she believes in the magic of ritual and in the triumph of hope. She doesn't think marriage is outdated or a form of servility for women. Her own marriage did not last but that has never soured her, either against the man or the institution. She doesn't know whether her own marital status makes her uniquely well or uniquely ill-qualified to judge the situation.

She says that when she speaks – *if* she speaks – the bride-to-be will cease to be her friend. Whatever happens, one way or the other, she will be out of their lives. If they marry, she will be excluded from everything except triumphant announcements of new babies, anniversaries and assurances of how wrong she was. If they do not marry, she will be held vaguely to blame for it all. So why speak?

Because her own friendship with the bride-to-be is not important, the girl's future is. Nobody else has had the guts to say anything except squeak about how romantic it is and how they're looking forward to the wedding. Even the conclave who say it's going to be a disaster are saying nothing. All the Courageous Wedding Guest is looking for is a set of words that doesn't sound patronising, hurtful or sour. Words that might make her look at the situation again.

She wondered did I have any help with those words.

None at all. They should never be said. A woman is just as entitled as a man to marry a dumbo – just as men say they have been doing for years. It might be a nice rest after work. That's what men always say.

PART III

ON KITH, KIN AND CLOSE ENCOUNTERS

A BLAST OF IT

*"People with a touch or a blast of arthritis love those
who don't talk about it, but do heed it . . ."*

I have got a lot of support from people who are going to
write torrents of abuse to Aer Rianta about their cavalier
attitude to people's legs. Since I complained about it, some
readers were kind enough to inquire if I had become an
invalid. The answer is no, but the Touch of Arthritis that
lurks in most of us who live in a damp country has become a
Blast of Arthritis.

I have a kind doctor who says that nobody ever died of it
and it has never appeared on a death certificate, which is
quite comforting in the reaches of the night when you think
you might well get new hips some day if you were to get
thinner. Weight, sadly, is no help, it would appear, in any
aspect of life except Sumo wrestling.

Most people with arthritis would prefer not to be greeted
with cries of amazement as they limp in. They would prefer
not to be asked: "What happened?" in tones of surprise and
sympathy because the answer – which is about the bones
gradually eroding with wear and tear – is a downer for
everyone: you feel they'd much prefer to hear that it was a
skiing accident, or that you had fallen out of bed with
someone entirely unsuitable.

So most of us who have it try to pretend, for as long as
possible, that we don't. I got quite good at that. It was a
matter of identifying litter bins that I could sit on if the walk
down a street was too long. Or railings to lean against,

pretending you were rooting in your handbag for something, and there are lovely little jutting out ledges on shop windows that you could sink onto – but sadly not enough of them.

Then, when you are indoors, you learn to find a high stool, like a bar stool. In my case, this is not difficult since I'm often in a bar anyway. But, if I were going to a reception in a hotel, I would ring in advance and ask could I have a bar stool set aside for me. Sometimes you hear a note of apprehension in their voices, as if you had been working your way north from Mizen Head, always having to order bar stools, but mainly they are co-operative.

If you are invited to someone's house for a stand-up gathering, you could ask them to lend you their kitchen stool. This can be a problem if the rest of the house is posh and the kitchen stool looks deeply shabby. I sometimes bring a shower cap to put on the stool which a hostess may be unwilling to produce – at least this way they look deliberately ludicrous rather than just tacky.

There are lots of ways to pretend that your two legs are working fine. Like being in places before other people, and then they only see you sitting down and think you are as right as rain. When leaving a dinner table, you must always remember to stand for a moment, deep in conversation with the other guests, before you head off, otherwise one of your legs could fail you and you're flat on the floor.

There are a hundred ways of making life better and a great many people who read this will have their ruses. It has nothing to do with foolish vanity, or wanting to look younger or stronger, it has a lot to do with well-meaning, non-arthritic people constantly, relentlessly, saying the wrong thing.

You can be sure that almost everyone who is able to read has heard of, and tried, capsules of concentrated mussel, particular vinegars, vitamin supplements, and seaweed baths. They have or haven't helped as the case may be, but we do not want every social gathering ruined with people holding forth on them. Maybe, if someone feels very strongly in favour of some cure, they could send a note rather than turning someone's house into an episode from *Casualty*.

Arthritis doesn't make you deaf. If you wonder whether someone can make the stairs, then ask that someone – don't ask his or her friends. Our hearing is still as good as ever, and our sensitivities are a little more sharp and prickly. If people talk as if we weren't there, we think that our touch of arthritis must be too terrible and hideous to acknowledge directly, but we are too far gone to notice if they speak of it in front of us.

Since my Touch became a Blast, I have got myself a beautiful beech folding stool. It's a lovely piece of furniture for a start, but the top folds down and you can carry it with you without looking as if you had come in with a van to move the contents of a building. I got mine made by Smyth Studios Cabinet Makers, 1a Stoneview Place, Dun Laoghaire, and it's extremely solid because Mr Smyth and I thought about the possibilities and dangers of an insubstantial folding stool, and they were too horrible to contemplate.

I love this stool: it fits in the boot of the car, in a taxi, it has been on the bus and a DART. I was showing it to someone proudly, and she said: "What a tragedy that you have to do that, but still, you're being brave." I wanted to pick up my beautiful stool and beat her senseless with it.

It is not tragic. It's very practical. I will have something to sit on. It's self-centred. I want to be the same height as everyone else when they are standing and I'm sitting so that I can take part in, and even dominate, the conversation.

People with a Touch or a Blast of arthritis love those who don't talk about it, but do heed it. Those who don't say that you're walking better this week than last week, as if they were tracing a toddler's steps, but who do manage to park near where you're going and always walk at your speed.

We don't want to hear of a marvellous man here or a great woman there, a diet of frogs' legs and sun-dried tomatoes, a prayer to someone with special intercession for inflamed joints – or that we should pull ourselves together and walk straighter. We're trying to do that. All the time, as it happens.

Most people who have arthritis know quite a lot about it, but it's only sensible to know as much as can be known, that's why we should all have a subscription to *Arthritis News*. It comes out four times a year, is full of sensible information, and you could always write to it yourself to make your own views felt.

You won't find anyone patronising you in this particular publication and it's well worth a fiver a year. Send to the Arthritis Foundation of Ireland, 1 Clanwilliam Square, Grand Canal Quay, Dublin 2.

INFIDEL IN-LAW

"Was it total hypocrisy to pretend that nothing had been seen . . . or was that the only sensible thing to do?"

We went to a restaurant in London which has so many plants it could be the set of *The Jungle Book*. You have to lift fronds out of your way in order to see whoever you are having lunch with, everyone else is masked in greenery and hanging foliage. The waiters hack their way through from time to time, but it's mainly a great place for a chat.

We were catching up on a lot: the death of a good friend, the unexpected niceness of someone who used to be impossible, the equally unexpected awfulness of a one-time soul mate, life in Dalkey, life in the part of the world she lives in, how I had become a cat bore, how she had become a grandmother.

One of the disadvantages of this place is that, when you have to go to the bathroom, you need a machete to get past the decor and then you'd be afraid you'd land back at the wrong table. When she came back she was so white I thought she must have been sick.

She wished it had been so simple. She had seen her son-in-law closeted behind some plants, holding the hand and nuzzling the cheek of a woman who was not his wife. This was the son-in-law spoken of only minutes before as being a workaholic who was at this present moment in New York, but who would be returning next weekend for a big family reunion and the birthday of his three-year-old son. My friend's grandson.

He had been spoken of in the warmest terms, sympathetically, with the hope that the world would settle down a bit and he wouldn't need to work so hard to provide for his family. And now the lying little sod had a fancy woman and wasn't in America at all. My friend looked as if she was going to faint. A waiter was found by radar through the greenery and a brandy ordered. She got a lot of homespun hopeless chat from me.

It might be someone who *looked* like him. No, it was his suit, his hair, his trendy briefcase with his leather jacket on the chair beside him. His wife might *know* he was back. He might have got in early this morning? No, she had been talking to her daughter just before lunch. The girl had said that the poor lamb was rushing from meeting to meeting and had left a message on the answering machine. He was so looking forward to the weekend.

I wondered would it have been a surprise? It was a surprise all right, my friend said grimly. Could it be an innocent lunch, I wondered. Lots of lunches are, maybe they had too much wine and grabbed each other's hands and said isn't this all wonderful? Our own pasts have been littered with such lunches. Haven't they?

"What you are doing," she said to me in a tone of steel, "is saying I should do nothing. That I should pretend to my daughter I didn't see him, that I should kiss him on both cheeks next weekend at the child's birthday and say how well he's looking." Glumly, I said that I thought it was better than the alternatives.

There was a silence. I longed for him to crash through the shrubbery shouting that it was all on *Candid Camera* and he had really fooled his mother-in-law hadn't he, and for his wife and the three-year-old to appear by his side. But even my fantasy life didn't take me far down that road.

We had been talking earlier about a woman we both knew who had been told that she was getting a promotion. But it was generally known that someone else was being groomed for the job. Her secretary had told her that, and thereby saved her face, her reputation. We had both been praising the secretary. It must have called for very great courage. She could have kept her head down. No one would have blamed her. But she had done a brave and honourable thing. The memory of the conversation hung between us in the air. Why was it different if it was your daughter? Why is it different if it is about love, not work?

It was all about dignity. No woman should be left in innocence thinking her husband was slaving away in New York while he was feeding his face in a London restaurant. But where was the dignity in telling something as humiliating as that? Was it not, possibly, the absolute denial of dignity? Would the girl ever be able to look at her mother again without remembering that her mother had been the bearer of bad news? And if she threw the guy out, wouldn't she sometimes, in the dark reaches of a lonely night, wish her mother had never told her?

Or, if she kept him and never referred to it, wouldn't she think that her mother despised her, or that her husband was at it again? And if she *did* bring up the matter of the lovey-dovey lunch with her husband, how edgy would that make family gatherings from now on?

If we had been talking about someone else's life or the plot of a novel, we would have found the topic interesting. A set of choices? Definitions even. Was it total hypocrisy to pretend that nothing had been seen, to be an ostrich, to let things take their own way? Or was that the only sensible thing to do? If he had gone to another restaurant. If we had gone to another restaurant. Useless wishes. We hadn't. He hadn't.

She said I had made her question other things in the past. Had I been devious on other occasions? Did I only care for the form and appearance of things? Was true friendship not about to survive confrontation about something as important as betrayal? She said she would not be judgmental, she would deliver the information and leave it for her daughter to act on or ignore as she wished. That was courage and love. What I would offer was papering over cracks and was timid and was probably part of the

Casanova's charter that allowed your men to go out and lech over lunches, sure and safe in the comfortable knowledge that woolly liberals like myself would keep their secrets.

Was that the solidarity of sisterhood, she wondered? Had the mellowness of maturity meant that I had got soft-centred? Like so many things these days, it remained unresolved.

And in my heart I know she will tell her daughter. And I am certain that she will be wrong.

Peace on Hearth

"In every peace-making gesture you have to recognise the rights and wrongs of the other party even though you think you have all the rights . . ."

If it can be attempted in Northern Ireland, in Israel and in Sarajevo, it can be tried in the home. It is heart-breaking to read the statistics about stress and rows in a season of too much expectation. Visitors from Mars would be very confused to hear of such hype and hope followed by heart attacks, family feuds and intensive consultation of marriage counsellors.

The number of people needing marital mediation or advice soars by 50 per cent in January as a direct result of the festive season, and whole budgets fall to pieces.

And, if we are to believe the doom brigade, all kinds of relationships fall apart at this time of year. Those who have been bereaved, divorced or separated find it a hell on earth, and even those who go into it quite good-naturedly find themselves snarling at siblings and at loggerheads with in-laws.

Who are these people? I have never known *anyone* fight with each other at Christmas. Fall asleep stuffed with food and drink, yes certainly, but fight?

Last week I met a woman who had a fight with her sister last Christmas. It poisoned the year and it has made her dread tomorrow, when they will all be gathering again in her mother's house where the row took place.

What was it about? Well, of all things, it was about Christmas crackers. It then moved on to the stuffing for the turkey.

Could she be serious?

Never more so, apparently.

She had brought crackers to the party. She had just rushed into a shop and bought them at the last moment. They had awful plastic toys in them, stupid riddles and hats that fell apart after ten seconds. Her sister had been scornful, very publicly. "That was all you had to do, get crackers, and look at what you turned up with," she said.

The woman was outraged. It was *not* all she had to do. She had a hell of a lot to do, like keep secret the fact that her husband was out of work; like drive everyone here and there in a falling-to-bits car; like go to a cemetery to put flowers on a grave; like be responsible for setting a table with a whole lot of different people's china and cutlery and get it all back to the right people; like keeping the fires going because nobody else ever noticed until they went out; like exercising the dog because otherwise he'd howl the house down; like keeping all the bones and putting them in a saucepan for her mother to make soup later – the rest of the family threw them out in reckless abandon.

And her sister said that the bloody crackers were all she had to do, the sister who put packet stuffing in the turkey.

Yes, cheap packet stuffing mixed with water. Dry as dust, you might as well have eaten the contents of the Hoover. It wasn't as if she didn't have the money. The new car stood gleaming outside the door. It wasn't as if she had all that much to do.

So the stuffing had been mentioned then? Criticised? It had. It wouldn't have been mentioned had the crackers not been mentioned . . .

But a whole year? Sisters who had been friends couldn't have fallen out for a year over this.

They had preserved the outward civilities. Smiles and waves at the First Communion, waves and smiles at Mother's birthday lunch, but they deliberately sat at different ends of the table.

Did their husbands know? Oh yes, but you know what men are like, they didn't think it was important. This year her sister is doing the crackers; probably got them from Harrods, she sniffs. And is she doing the stuffing? No, that would be petty, someone else is. She's doing the plum pudding.

There was a time when these sisters laughed over things together, and went out to the kitchen for a cigarette and confided things, and wondered was their sister-in-law pregnant again and whether their mother would like a proper worktop in the kitchen or if she actually loved all these different heights and surfaces. There was a time when they used to giggle over Christmases long ago, when their father was alive and when he drank the brandy that was meant to pour over the pudding. When they held on to each other sentimentally as they watched their toddlers under the tree and said life was wonderful. And now they are miles apart because of some insane Christmas tension that built up last year.

I advised her to write a note to her sister. I nearly wrote it for her. Something like "I was such a stupid fool last year, all that fuss over crackers and stuffing, when all I wanted to do, like everyone else on earth, was have a happy Christmas. I hope it will be happy this year and I'm sorry for my part in whatever nonsense went on before. All my love."

She thinks not. She thinks that she didn't begin it. If she had started it, then, maybe.

But what about their children, their mother? They must be aware of the coldness; it will contribute a frost to the celebration.

Oh go on, I said to her, of course, the letter's a bit hypocritical. In every peace-making gesture you have to recognise the rights and wrongs of the other party, even though you think you have all the rights and they are permanently in the wrong.

Her sister will weep out gratitude and embrace her. Or she'll grudgingly and brusquely say, yes, the hatchet should be buried. Or she will behave like a sewer-house rat and say she herself was in no way to blame for what happened, in which case this woman will have virtue and goodness on her side for the rest of her days and need never feel guilty again. But she has to take the step. Otherwise she is adding to the statistics that say this is a time when families fall out.

Home Truths

"Remember how many youngsters there are living in squalor in bed-sits . . . why should we not accept that at the other end of the age curve similar feelings exist?"

Of course she would be much better off in a home. Everyone knows that. There would be no danger of electrocuting herself, gassing herself, falling over the small stool, scalding her wrist with the boiling water.

She would be less anxious in a home; she would not worry about shadows across the windows being intruders. She would have no fears about knocks on the door late at night. Sounds of suspicious cars or creaking boards. She would have *company* in a home.

She spends long hours of the day and evening alone at the moment. She would be in a place where there were other people to talk to. She could pick and choose those she liked and those she didn't. No longer would she be dependent on the accident of who lived on either side of her.

Her daughter and son-in-law think the time they would spend visiting her in a home would be good time. It wouldn't be a series of bolstering up a tottering system – trying to exclude draughts, re-position chairs, clean grime from surfaces, change her out of food-stained garments and persuade her that she would be far better off in care.

If she were being looked after, then the time they would have with her would be – to use that terrible expression – Quality Time. They wouldn't have to waste so many hours on inessentials, and circular arguments that are beginning to destroy all the love that has been there up to now.

They are a loving family. The daughter would, and does, do anything for her mother, a woman who made a lot of sacrifices in her own youth so that the daughter should have a good start. Her mother has committed no crime except to turn 88 and become a bit feeble. That, and express a wish to hold on to her own home.

The son-in-law loves her too. She championed his cause 35 years ago when he was considered an unsuitable match and his future father-in-law had dismissed him as a degenerate Teddy Boy. Her son-in-law doesn't want to tidy this woman away just for convenience. He genuinely thinks it would make her a much happier and more contented person to be in a place where a cup of tea was handed to her and didn't involve a hazardous series of movements.

He thinks it's just a matter of their deciding on the move and then waiting for the dust to settle. She can't be really and truly attached to a house that is causing her nothing but hassle. She knows they'll never abandon her, that she'll see the grandchildren regularly. Her only other child, a son who lives abroad, would be even more eager to come home with his family if he thought that Mother was nice and clean and warm and safe in a place where she didn't worry about everything from gurgles in the tank to whether the television licence has been paid.

This son-in-law is a kind man with a fistful of brochures, a man who has done his sums and wants his mother-in-law to be settled and his wife to come out of what he calls the screaming heebie jeebies. He says that 80 per cent of their conversation now is spent talking about The Situation.

Every phone call causes them to jump in case it is news of some disaster that they feel they could have prevented. The daughter, who is in her late 50s, tells me that her mother would never knowingly upset the family and that this is an additional dilemma. If everything were different, she can almost hear her mother's voice advising consideration and practicality. But of course everything is not different and she has to play the parent now. A role she cannot act because always her mother's own goodness intervenes and she feels nothing but guilt. Then she gets angry and she gets more guilty still.

And she says to me that I don't understand and she's right. Our parents died so young that they remain for ever in the mind as the young, healthy, strong people they were. I don't know how I would cope with the problem that so many of my friends are facing.

So you might not understand from the inside but you can sympathise. You can imagine yourself in each situation. I imagine myself as the daughter and, because I'm of a bossy nature, I can see myself making huge efforts at persuasion. I would hate it but I would be so sure that it was for the best in the end that I would grit myself to all the pain and dismantling of a mother's life for her own good. Then, for a moment, I imagine myself as the mother. We know what it's like to be young and foolish and vulnerable and awkward . . . because we've been through that. We haven't *been* old yet. We don't know what it's like.

It might have an awful lot to do with feeling safe in the familiar. And being prepared to put up with any amount of inconvenience, and even downright discomfort, to hang on in. Remember how many youngsters there are living in squalor in bed-sits, with hopeless heating, disgusting plumbing and having to hike up and down four flights of stairs with peeling wallpaper. We can all accept *that* as a rite of passage, a need for independence, even though a much more comfortable alternative exists in the parents' house. Why should we not accept that, at the other end of the age curve, similar feelings exist?

I advise the couple to stand back a bit. Although things are not perfect, they are so much better than they used to be. The mother could have a home help morning and afternoon. A nurse can come to wash her on certain days of the week, meals on wheels can be delivered.

Her daughter and son-in-law should not be there every single day, maybe every second day. Good humour should be maintained, even in the face of negative thinking. We were all fairly negative when we were young and being looked after. Our parents never complained that, for the first years of life, we were not rational about things like our nutrition and lifestyle. We must owe them a similar tolerance at the other end, even if they aren't all gurgling and sweet and adorable, like babies and toddlers are.

I know, I know. I have friends whose elderly parents distort what they say, who imagine grudges and grievances where none exists. I have friends with a mother who suspects their motives and thinks they are just waiting to sell the house over her head, or move into it. Nothing could be further from the truth, or indeed from her mind, were she more rational and less frail. It must be almost impossible to see the woman who was strong and independent, who helped you to mould your life, become frail, difficult, querulous and ultimately manage to turn your love for her into exasperation.

But I think we have to ask honestly, who we are doing it for when we insist that the excellent nursing home is the answer?

When my elderly neighbour in London was in a hospital

ward for the elderly, I loved it. I loved it to bits. She was clean and pink and well fed and cared for. I didn't have to come home and know that she was there next door, terrified of intruders, unkempt and unable to do anything in a house she could hardly see. But she didn't love it. She was aching to be home. As soon as her hip mended, back she went to the entirely unsuitable house.

Then came the day, too late by many people's standards, when she was ready to go in. And she went.

It must be a heartbreak for anyone seeing a mother in that position. But I truly believe you must wait until she wants to go.

SCANDALOUS LIAISONS

"I am sick to death of hearing about affairs. There is nothing as boring as a lover unless you are the lover"

There's a friend of mine who is very exercised these days about a rumour that is flying around Dublin suggesting that two people are having an affair with one another. One is well-known and the other is married. I must have heard it five times, accompanied by deep authoritative, confirming nods from people who more or less implied that they have been secreted away at every location where intimacy is Taking Place, as they used to say in old-fashioned divorce cases.

Now I'm as interested as the next person in unusual information of this sort. But only for about two minutes and then, to be honest, my interest flags. If they are having an affair, so what? They must know all the drama that discovery would cause. Perhaps that is actually part of the heightened excitement of it. They must know that there are people they are hurting and, undoubtedly, they will have taken their own view of that. Either this love is bigger than both of them, or else life can be compartmentalised. There are endless ways of rationalising things, we all know that. Or perhaps it is all out in the open and they have told everyone that matters, so there's no need for whispering. Soon it will be public knowledge.

But my friend tells me a new, and as yet unvoiced, opinion. She says this story is just not true. She knows both of them. It is a modern myth, a stone that has gathered so much moss that it is now unrecognisable. What is more, she tells me, the two people involved haven't a notion of what is being said about them. And she wonders what she should do.

Nothing, I say, before she finishes her sentence.

But this can't be right, she says. What kind of friend would stand by and let the dogs in the street discuss the details of an affair which is not taking place? And she is a good friend of one of the people and a good acquaintance of the other. Shouldn't she tell them what everyone is saying? For their own sake, she pleads.

Well I should hope it is for their own sake, not just for hers, in case she is tempted to play God. Who else's sake would it be for? But I still think she would be out of her skull to mention it at all. Let her look at the options.

She comes in with her I-think-you-ought-to-know message: the Whole Country is talking about them. Trailing clouds of unpleasantness, it brings with it the discovery of wrongful accusations.

If they are not having an affair, they are thrown into a

welter of maddened outrage at the unfairness of it. They will want chapter and verse, they will demand to know who said what and where and under what circumstances. Writs will get underway, litigation will begin, apologies will be demanded. The helpful friend will be standing out in front of the firing line without a bullet-proof vest. She will get all the accusations redirected at her. She will be asked why it took her so long to tell, why she hadn't alerted them earlier. There will be tears, recriminations and endless shouting about the world having a sick mind. Whatever happened to the idea of a platonic friendship, they might well ask?

Suppose they *are* having an affair.

She is the messenger bringing the bad news, the news that they are not invisible. They will tell her that she is small-minded to listen to such tittle-tattle, and they will want to know what her response was every time she heard the rumour. If she says that she always denied it (which is true), then they might well laugh and say she is an eejit. Or they might say she should have told them earlier, to mark their cards for them. *Whatever* she does will be the wrong thing.

But how cowardly, how weak, she says, to stay out of something because it might make you unpopular. She wouldn't have thought I would have followed this line. Well, when someone puts it to you like that, you have to ask yourself why you take a view that an honourable person considers cowardly.

I think it is because I am sick to death of hearing about affairs. There is nothing as boring as a lover unless you *are* the lover, as if it was all mint new and no one else has ever experienced it before.

And, as everybody knows, people having an affair

positively *thrive* on the excitement of whether anyone knows or everyone knows or some people do and some people don't. Even if they don't admit it.

I couldn't have cared less about all these Antonia de Sanchas and Bienvenida Buck-types, except to worry mildly about what they are going to do next. I felt a bit sorry for David Mellor's wife and for Sir Anthony Buck, since they were both betrayed. I felt no pity for Alan Clark, who is just so boastful and indiscreet, or for the silly judge and his silly family who are greedy and naïve, nor for Alan Clark's wife with a face carved with lines of forgiveness and understanding.

None of what we read about them has anything to do with the truth. It is all exaggerated out of recognition and the Chinese whispers of rumours have been made even more grotesque by the paid publicists and the tabloids vying to buy their exclusives. If they were left smartly alone, they'd all go home on the 6.30 and eat their tea like good boys and girls. Of course they would, if no-one was interested in them. The greatest disservice you could do to them is to tell them that nobody cares. Lights would go out all over the place if they ceased to be centre stage.

And so I think all this has something to do with the rumour that's going around Dublin and the huge attention it's getting. I think my friend would be quite wrong and would be in serious danger of becoming a dopey Drama Queen if she were to approach the Main Players and tell them what she felt they ought to know.

The very best thing to do, if she has their best interests at heart, is to ignore it. She should start a one-woman movement appealing to people not to get over-excited about unlikely pairings along the strange and rocky road through life. Her best service would be to direct less, rather than more, light on what may or may not be happening.

They are old enough to play with the big boys and girls in the real world. If they are just good pals and not having the steamy affair that the whole place is talking about then they must be deaf and blind. I advise my friend to let them get on with it or not to get on with it, as the case may be. She can do nothing but harm by opening her mouth.

If she is still really concerned she could rely on the old, anonymous letter trick, or send them this column postmarked from the GPO. Cowardly.

Moi?

PHONE PHOBIA

"There are enough things to be afraid of in life without setting up the poor old telephone as a source of possible terror"

My friend has a very bright eight-year-old daughter. She has taught her to answer the phone with the word "Hello". She says it's very dangerous to give your number when you answer the phone.

Dangerous to give your own phone number when someone has rung it? I wondered whether we were all in danger of living out Operation Fort Knox fantasies. But no, she insists, that's what Telecom Eireann advises you to do. Read the leaflet, she says, aggrieved. And it's true, it *does* say that on the leaflet, and it urges you to advise children specifically to follow that procedure.

And if someone asks you "What number is this?" you mustn't tell them, you must ask them what number they are looking for and then say triumphantly that they've got the wrong one.

I *suppose* Telecom feels it's protecting people from what they call the Irish Burglars Association, and trying to cut down on the Heavy Breathers, who might accidentally fumble on a female answering a phone, and keep the number forever as a place to ring and torture with grunts and obscenities.

And in theory this is good. Good that they should care enough about subscribers to want them not to be hassled. But isn't it also dangerous to manoeuvre us all into the position that the sound of a ringing telephone becomes like a scene in a Hitchcock drama? Something that will widen the eyes, constrict the throat and set the nerves a-jangle.

There are enough things to be afraid of in life without setting up the poor old telephone as a source of possible terror.

My friend's daughter has been warned to give no information whatsoever. This seems to me to be a retrograde step.

When I was eight the great emphasis was to state the number clearly and make sure you found out who was speaking and told them when your parents were going to be home. There was no greater crime in the book than to report "Someone rang". All right, so the world has moved on, and you don't want encourage children to babble that they are Home Alone. But is it good for them to be told that they must "never answer any questions on the phone, no matter how innocent they seem, unless you know the caller"?

This is in heavy type in Telecom's leaflet, and my friend is busy warning and warning her child about it. She thinks that this is the way safety lies, that this way she will prevent the girl from ever coming across something unpleasant and unsettling.

I advise her to give up this set of instructions. You can't protect anyone from hearing unpleasant things, and if you give a child too many rules and regulations, some are bound to fall out of the system. I'd prefer an eight-year-old to be told morning noon, and night about the traffic, and not to be wandering into it, rather than waste two minutes on the dangers that might lurk on the other end of the phone.

All very well for you, my friend says, you are a big confident woman. No one ever rang you and said things that frightened you.

Of course they did. And of course I didn't like it. But I am sure that it was much better to have been given the background information that people who had to do that were (a) in the minority and (b) not the full shilling. No one ever told me to fear the phone. I was certainly told that if anyone started on a spiel of the objectionable sort, you said nothing, you gasped not at all, and you hung up as soon as possible.

Some people said to nuisance callers: "Hold on a minute, I'm just getting the tape recorder." Others said: "This call is being traced and there's a fine *and* a jail sentence so you'd better make the most of it." And if someone rang persistently and never spoke you could always have the number changed. It costs £18.56 (including VAT) to get a new number, but if there was a weirdo constantly ringing you it might be worth it.

The friend does not agree. I am speaking from a position of so-called maturity, she thinks. A child must be taught to shield herself; much more sinister people are about nowadays – prevention is better than having to cope.

But how can it be good for a child's psyche, just as she is about to come to the serious telephoning decade of her life – to be told that out there is a bunch of nutters and potential robbers and violators and she must give no information when she answers the phone?

Her friends will be ringing, for heaven's sake, and her parents' friends, and people giving information, wanting information, visitors passing through calling to say Hi from the airport. There will be bosom pals who have had rows with their mothers, needing consolation, older pals who have lost their Love and needing even deeper consolation. There may be news that she has won a raffle, got her Leaving, had a positive or negative pregnancy test . . . and for the rest of her life she will have been trained to answer a phone cautiously, giving no information in case abusers lurk out there.

I am all for giving and getting information. I *love* people who answer their phones with their name or their number. The world is much more of a jungle if we make it one, and it is definitely a regression if you fear to say who you are and what number is written on your telephone.

Telecom is trying to be helpful, but I genuinely think it is just creating further alarm. They tell you truthfully in the leaflet that they can't trace nuisance calls without being asked to do so by the Gardaí. The Gardaí say that, if there's a series of abusive or threatening calls, people usually know or suspect what quarter they're coming from and so action can be taken at that end. And in the case of unexplained calls, the number change is always advised.

So why frighten the eight-year-old? Why sit down and tell her that there are Bad Men ringing up, watching the house, wanting to know Daddy and Mummy's business?

There has to be some humour as well as sympathy for those who use the phone to gain a thrill. A friend who smokes a great deal too many cigarettes and has a deep voice answered her phone the other day, and the desperate caller took her for a man. Disappointed that he couldn't unfurl his invective, he did the next best thing.

"Your wife's a slag," he said excitedly, "she does it with anyone." If he wasn't cured of his little problem by the laughter he got, he never will be.

He certainly didn't call again that evening.

Split Ends

"The best friends are the ones who let you tell the story,
over and over, until you have decided what you must do"

You could hear the sigh of relief for three counties. She has thrown him out. It is not another feminist cry of triumph that yet another dirty, stinking rat has been given his marching orders. This was a very unhappy scene. The woman loved far too deeply and put up with so much from the man that he could be excused for thinking that he really was something special, and someone from whom no one expected the normal courtesies of life.

Over a period of years those who knew them have watched astounded, wondering how much more she would take. Even if anyone wanted to, there would have been no point in telling her about any of his countless infidelities, in some misplaced belief that you thought she ought to know.

She knew. She knew them all.

They did not have children; she wasn't staying with him

to keep the home together. These are the Nineties; she didn't stay because to leave would have meant being cast adrift with no one to support her. It isn't a society that looks oddly at the separated. In fact, her situation was much more odd the way it was. But she stayed – until Christmas. And on Christmas Eve, suddenly, in the middle of Grafton Street with everyone filled with Christmas cheer and happiness – linking up with their loved ones and going in to have a drink with people they met – she caught sight of her face in a shop window . . . and saw that she looked like an illustration for some article called *Unhappiness*.

It was as if she had been given a chance to look at herself from the outside. She came home and she told him that their marriage was over. He said that her timing was spectacular. He didn't say that he loved her, or wanted her to stay; he didn't promise to change his ways, limit his extracurricular activity, refrain from humiliating her in public. He concentrated on the very inappropriate way she had approached the subject, and how it was rather typical of her to balls up the season of goodwill.

He went off and imposed on friends for Christmas, she stayed in their home and cried her eyes out.

She moved into her sister's house and sat stunned, waiting for and getting all the solidarity she knew would be forthcoming from her friends.

I advised them to tread warily, very warily indeed. They think she wants huge bolstering support, the firming up of her resolution by the recitation of more and more of his dirty tricks. They are not going to confirm her in the rightness of her decision by defining still further his villainy. This is only going to make her feel foolish, vulnerable, and let her believe that for years she had been an object of great pity, if not actual scorn.

I advise her closest friend not to start talking about getting a tough lawyer and taking the guy for everything he's got. This is not the language of survival; it's the dialogue of revenge. Of course she needs to be told that she must value herself, and not underestimate her part in the company that she and her husband once had, but companies can be dissolved without blood on the floor.

Her best friend doesn't agree. She says I am shilly-shallying over it all, that I have no courage because I fear they will get back together and I don't want to be seen as someone who sat in judgement. I don't want to be the worst in the world. Up to a point.

They *might* get back together. That woman put up with so much, for so long, that she must love him in a way we don't understand. Or sort of love him. It couldn't have been just fear or inertia on her part that kept the thing going.

But that's not the real point. The real point is that not only is it too soon to dance on the grave of a love that is finished, it's a dangerous thing to do anyway.

Are her friends going to be there all the time? At night, when she returns to an empty house? She will not live with her sister forever, she doesn't have another relationship in mind and it's hard to see her treading the path towards finding one.

Will they be there not just at the beginning to see her over the first bit, but in a few months' time which may be the worst bit? The time when they think she should have pulled herself together and got on with things.

Will they include her in everything they are doing, going to the pictures, the theatre, having supper, and will they be able to do it without patting her on the head?

That is what real friendship is about, much, much more than telling her she is well out of it and advising her to retain the high ground and fight him to the Court of Human Rights if necessary. Her relationship and her marriage had some good elements in it. There were times when they were happy. Both of them. It was not all a matter of dependency and doormat behaviour. She must be allowed to recall those good elements without the pack of supporters starting to panic and seeing signs of the old order returning.

Anyone making such a huge decision must not be pushed to it by the well-meaning efforts of friends who, after all, are either safe within relationships that do work, or are already single or separated. She might well think that she was being patronised by the former, or over-encouraged by the latter.

The best friends are the ones who let you tell the story over and over again until *you* have decided what you must do. There is nobody who finds that advice harder to act on than myself, but I know that it is true.

WILLPOWER

"Nobody ever died from making a will. But a lot of people have left a hell of a lot of confusion behind by not making one . . ."

We heard an item on the radio about Make Your Will Week, urging people to drop into Buswell's Hotel and meet fleets of lawyers who would tell them how simple the process was. Then, during the week of the promotion, people could make a will for the relatively low cost of £25.

The man curled his lip and looked at the radio with pure hate.

"Don't solicitors give you the dry heaves?" he said, assuming my complete agreement. "As if they hadn't enough money already, they're trying to frighten poor, harmless, perfectly healthy passers-by and scare the life out of them with Testaments and Sound Minds and advice about what to do with my ashes."

He was totally serious. He was a married man of 38 years of age who hadn't a notion of making a will, and what's more, thought that it was like inviting bad luck, illness or an air crash to do anything of the sort.

He received the news that I had been making wills cheerfully and healthily for over 30 years with disbelief, and not a little distaste. He thought it was arrogant, with distinct overtones of the Grande Dame, or owner of the mill – reminiscent of an eccentric Aunt Agatha, power-crazed and disinheriting everyone around her on whim.

But of course this is idiotic. I made my first will when I was 21 and had £100 and I see no association whatsoever with making wills and dying. I see a lot of connection, however, between not making wills and leaving a monumental cock-up for other people to deal with. Solicitors do not give me the dry heaves but people who are too mean to employ one, and therefore render a will invalid, do.

The history of litigation is strewn with shoddy home-made wills, usually beginning with the phrase "If I die", instead of "When I die" or "After my death". A reality check for those who begin a serious statement of intent with the words "If I die" needs to be considered. What about the alternative?

"Suppose I am, by chance, one of the few, or indeed the only human being, who doesn't die, then let this document be null and void."

People who make home-made wills have often invalidated them by trying to write everything on one page, so that when it eventually comes to probate, the court literally cannot read it and it is put aside.

They say "my money" when they don't mean money, they mean "estate". They give away more than they have, instead of dealing with the whole thing in percentages.

They disregard the provisions of the Succession Act and forget that the ratio of what they have actually by law belongs to a spouse. They leave bequests to people, bequests that are so vague that they cause endless and sometimes painful confusion. "I leave a chair and a decanter to my old friend." What chair? What decanter?

I gave this man the benefit of my blinding clarity and sureness that this was a matter in which right was on my side – and not on his.

He accused me of being a foolish lackey, an unpaid public relations officer for a profession which he likened to several tanks of barracudas. They weren't doing this for any one's *good* he said, astonished at my naïveté. They just wanted to make more money.

They weren't going to turn into very fat barracudas at £25 a will, I answered. This conversation had by now become highly confrontational.

Aha, he said, this offer was only to get you to put your toe in the water. Once they had got you in, taken your £25 and made your Simple Will, they would explain how you'd need to update it and come back every year or any time you coughed or sneezed. You would be in the system, making a will at every new moon or fluctuation of the Dow Jones Index.

He said it was ghoulish to try and persuade people of his

age to come in and discuss death. Perhaps I'd love it if groups of undertakers also had a promotion week, he said, and we could all go and be measured for coffins and choose nice inscriptions for our Celtic crosses.

If he *were* to die suddenly, well, what he had would go to his wife. That's what he'd like. Well, he wouldn't like it because he wouldn't like to be killed but it would be an okay way for his money to go.

So why then let all the solicitors trade in their small cars for big ones just to render the situation the way it was? Why should he go every few weeks and give some lawyer fistfuls of cash so that his wife would get all his money anyway? The whole business was insane.

Had he any friends, I asked him through gritted teeth. Had he parents, colleagues at all? Was there ever any cause he considered worthy of support? Any youngster whose education might be helped by a contribution? Any token to be handed over with a pleasing remark?

This wasn't the point, he said. It was a point, I insisted. A very important point. I showed him the typewriter, the bound books and the little glass left to me by friends in their wills. He is young and he thinks I am a combination of melodramatic, sentimental and naïve – is there any worse mixture?

But he did seem to be thinking about it.

Why should the barracudas who were manning the booths in the hotel during Make a Will Week get all the £25 cheques, he wanted to know? Wasn't that stealing work from brother barracudas? We checked. This is not the situation. The barracudas in the hotel give free advice, and urge people to go back to their own solicitors for the £25-a-head offer.

He was genuinely afraid that it might call the attention of the Fates, or whatever, as if someone up there would hear you making a will and consider it was time to haul you in. Did it not give me intimations of someone walking on my grave? he asked. And he was the one who thought me naïve. He probably doesn't walk on cracks on the road either.

My friend Mary Kotsonouris, in her book *Talking to your Solicitor*, says that, apart from in the occasional Agatha Christie story, nobody ever died from making a will. But a lot of people have left a hell of a lot of confusion behind by not making one. And they have left their friends unaware of how much they were valued.

That alone makes me advise healthy young people to get over their superstitions and do the thing nice and briskly, when the prospect of death is still ages away. Surely that kind of thinking couldn't drag you down and make you feel old before your time?

FOUL-WEATHER FRIEND

"What would really cheer her up would be if I were to say that I was in bad form"

I know someone who only comes to life when you tell her bad news. She is a real Cassandra, who likes to hear tales of woes and get to grips with them. The trouble is, she is a terrific sympathiser, and she specialises in grouses, gripes and situations where someone has been hard done by. So, if you have any huff or grievance or sense of being passed over, she's your woman. But dare to get better, to recover your good humour sufficiently to see things more lightheartedly, or from the other point of view, and the light goes out of her eyes. She is not a fair-weather friend, she is a foul-weather friend and I think people like that can be dangerous for your emotional health. They keep the barometer low long after it should have started to rise.

These are the kind, interested listeners who will remember, months later, how someone had cut you dead, long after you had forgotten it yourself; they will recall how hurt you were by somebody in power, someone whom you now like and do not associate with some gross injustice committed years ago.

I was pleased that someone I knew ages ago got a great job recently. Now, when I say ages ago, I am talking, not years, but decades. I said wasn't it grand that he had done so well, and the downbeat person said it was very generous of me to say that, considering the way he had stood me up that time.

A dark cloud floated over my head like one of those incomprehensible maps from the Met office. A vague, woolly memory came back to me of a night spent waiting and a lot of ultimately unsatisfactory explanation and counter-explanation. Had it ever been properly resolved, I wondered? Was he really suitable for his present position of importance, having played fast and loose with people in the past?

Was I in fact trying to suppress this memory myself, and had my pathetic pleasure in his appointment been some kind of inner cry?

Now, it was generous, in a way, for her to have remembered that incident. In a way. I must have told her about it and must have been delighted at the time, with the sympathetic response, the ready shoulder and the listening ear. At the time.

Does it make me a shallow person and a false confidante, if I didn't really want this incident filed away for twenty-something years and then trotted out again as one of the many catastrophic things that had happened to me in my life? Why did she never seem able to bring up the good times, the day her first article was published; the day my first article was published . . . these are the golden days carved in stone, why not think about them as much as the days we were rejected or others got garlands we thought should have been ours? Why not remember the day when we went to lunch with a drunken PR person who said he would put a fiver for each of us on a horse and it won at eight to one? *That* was a day. Memory can be selective, and perhaps there is a Pollyanna aspect to some of us that is equally unhealthy, tinting the glasses through which we view other days to a sickly shade of rose.

Perhaps this woman feels she is right to be aggrieved. She soldiered through the slights, the upsets and the insults and now we want to deny that such intimacy existed over what could now seem fairly irrelevant, even *petty* complaints.

Perhaps right is on her side. She was there when people needed a supportive, non-judgmental listener. She would still be there, and *is* there, I know, for anyone who has a sad story to tell. But she is not there for anyone who has a jolly story to tell. She brings you down – right down – unless you feed her compulsion to know the bad news.

You can't say you're fine or great or be cheerful if she asks how you are. You have to say something low-key, otherwise it's a non-conversation. If she were to ring now, and I were to say that things were fine and I had a lovely Easter, or that I was looking forward to friends coming to visit, there would be a silence. Then I would ask about her Easter and she would say it had been all right but the weather had been terrible. And I would say the weather had been terrible in Ireland too and I would hear her brightening a bit.

But what would really cheer her would be if I were to say that I was in bad form. Then she would ask why and I could say it was hard to know, really. And I would get the warmth of her interest and concern. To fuel the fire, I might add that I was full of arthritis and she would glow with sympathy and later I would hear from someone else that I am on all fours with it and isn't it a tragedy. If she asked about Kenya, I wouldn't say it was great because of the climate. I don't want to live in Kenya, I just want to go there on holiday. So I'd have to say it was a bit too hot for a holiday, which is a lie.

Most of the things I say to this kind, good woman are lies. So I talk to her less and less. I cannot bring myself to recall some of the low spots in her life and to remind her of humiliations and failures. I cannot believe that she would want to be led back to this territory. If we end up resolving to be downhearted in order to chime in with someone else's mood, it becomes a self-fulfilling prophecy. We *will* be downhearted. In the pits, in fact. And that's not going to help the planet or those who live on it.

Why should we have to say that the current suspension of violence is useless if we have some hope that it might lead to something? Why be forced to say things are fair-to-middling when things are fine? I'm not doing it anymore and I advise anyone else with Cassandra-like friends to take the same stand.

GIVING THANKS

*"You can't write the script. You can't give a gift and
make it into a deal"*

It doesn't have to be a long letter, the woman says, just a few
lines. A postcard even. Just something to say that the
children enjoyed it. To acknowledge that it happened.

It's not that she feels a martyr about giving them treats.
She *loves* to see them – she'll take them to pantomimes, or
to McDonalds, for as long as she has the strength and they
have the interest. She will leave them everything she has
when she dies anyway, whether they send her thank-you
letters or not.

But she thinks it's *such* a bad training not to make
children respond to generosity with some kind of gesture: a
drawing when they're very young, and then they could
graduate to a few words. It doesn't come naturally to children;
she remembers the difficulty she had with her own. But soon
it became like clockwork. Almost a Pavlovian response.

She would provide the paper and the envelope and the
stamp and her children were highly regarded as being very
polite. Not hypocritical little creeps, she thinks, just warm-
hearted and able to say they enjoyed something.

So what happened to all this politeness that she instilled?
Evidently it didn't last into the next generation.

No. But, she repeats, it's not a thing that they'd know for
themselves – they have to be told. And she doesn't like to
tell them. She doesn't want to say at the end of a perfect
day: "Now, if you enjoyed that you must write me a letter to
thank me."

But on the other hand she fears that if *somebody* doesn't tell them that, they might well grow up selfish, taking everything for granted. Or alternatively people will *think* that is what they are, since there will be no evidence otherwise.

She doesn't know if she should say something to their parents. After all, her son is very busy – he has a demanding job, he's away from home a lot. And for all this new equality and sharing the roles, it's not up to a man to organise thank-you letters, is it?

There's the danger that he might just snap at her and say she's old-fashioned and outdated. She doesn't feel very old at 58, but everything is relative. And he might see a veiled criticism of his wife in this too. She doesn't want to be a troublemaker.

That's why she has said nothing to her daughter-in-law. She has always been aware how prickly this relationship could be: her own mother-in-law had been less than sensitive over three decades ago. She hasn't forgotten. She has always been full of praise for how well her grandchildren are being brought up: it's only this one aspect that gets to her, because she sees it as much more important than the actual letter-writing itself.

Has she given any hints that she would like to see thank-you letters incorporated in their lifestyles? Oh yes, heavy hints. When she sends a present she will telephone to wonder has it arrived. She will be assured that it has. And did they like it, she will wonder? Oh, but they loved it, she will be promised, and sometimes they will be brought to the phone to tell Granny what a success it was.

If she has the grandchildren over to her house and a neighbour does something nice for them, she will suggest that they all write a letter. The thing that drives her mad is that her two little grandchildren seem to enjoy creating this letter with her. They will even add bits of news of their own about their goldfish. It's not as if they would find it a chore.

Is her daughter-in-law thoughtful and polite in other ways? Yes, very. That's the maddening thing. She's charming. No, no, I must believe her; this is not the classic case of a woman thinking that no other woman is good enough for her son. She has made an excellent home for her family and is most welcoming to the grandmother. She has a part-time job now and will not return to full-time work until the children are older. No way has she blotted her copybook, apart from this business of the bread-and-butter letters.

I know a lot of young mothers who would think that life is fairly crowded enough for children these days: there are so many things that they *have* to do already, that they don't want to add to them.

They wouldn't for example, think that something enjoyable like a treat with the grandmother should immediately have to be followed by the downside of it all: The Duty Letter.

Might there not be an argument in favour of keeping the whole thing pleasurable? No. She won't buy this. "It's all right for you," she says. "You don't have grandchildren. You don't know how lovely it is to get little letters from them."

I *do* know how great it is to hear from children. I've kept children's letters for years because they are such a pleasure.

But you can't write the script. You can't give a gift and make it into a deal. I give this to you and you give me the promise of a thank-you letter which will warm my heart. Either it will come or it won't. It will be inspired by a parent of course but, if that's not the way the household works, you have to accept it.

If you live with someone who never says "I love you" and you beg him or her to use those words, explaining how important it is to hear them, you would need to have a fairly short memory if the words suddenly thrilled you to the marrow with their spontaneity when they were delivered on demand.

I advise this woman not to say a word to her busy son, her admirable daughter-in-law and her much-loved grandchildren. I advise her from my own experience of sending a Christmas gift last year to two children in England from Australia; I genuinely thought it might have got lost. So I telephoned afterwards to know if they had got it, and they had, and it was all bad news because we can't do a thing for them now without the immediate and lengthy letter which is the product of parents' guilt and very possibly children's great rage.

I will never be able to read anything from them again with the same delight as before, because I know it's brought about by my having more or less said that I had expected to hear from them. I might as well write myself thank-you letters and open them on appropriate occasions.

So that's what I advise this woman to do. Ask for nothing because it will be dust in her mouth when it does arrive.

She should have faith in people's nature as well as in the training they get.

Perhaps when these children get a bit older they'll realise how much we all love to be thanked for things. And they'll do it all on their own. Their letters will then be much more meaningful than a box full of gratitude drawn from them by duty, extracted like teeth.

EMIGRANT'S RETURN

*"One of our own gone for three or four years was the
one who had least permission to criticise"*

He is 26 now, and he came home for Christmas and New
Year. Not an entirely successful visit. He doesn't quite know
why. He sat at the airport puzzling about it. It wasn't the
usual thing you hear about, like his parents treating him like
a kid or anything. No, they didn't cross-question him about
where he had been or what time he came home or anything.
They didn't smother him, make him feel claustrophobic, beg
him to go for interviews here to get a job, any job in Ireland,
like other people's parents did.

But it wasn't satisfactory.

Everyone has got very blinkered here, he thinks, smug,
self-satisfied. You can't say a thing against Ireland but
they're all bristling like a herd of hedgehogs. They all react
on cue if you say anything at all that is less than a hymn of
praise to the whole nation.

Take the streets. He made a comment, an ordinary
comment, about the litter and the way people throw
wrapping papers on the ground. He saw someone emptying
an ashtray out of a window and he just mentioned it, drew
attention to it just as you would to such a happening. But it
was taken as criticism.

And the beggars. He said it was terrible to see children
begging on the streets with little cardboard boxes. Well! You
should have heard the response. It was as if he had called
down the wrath of nations on the country.

He was told that there were many, many homeless sleeping in the streets of the particular part of the New World where he had gone to seek his fortune. He was reminded sharply by his sister that this was not a new phenomenon and they had always been there, so it did not do him any credit to notice it only since he had been away.

It was the same if he spoke with anything except awe about the meals when they dined out. He said that the service was indifferent in one place, the waiter shruggy, the wine waiter supercilious, that those people wouldn't last two minutes where he lived. The night was ruined for everyone. They said this was one of the best places in Dublin, that Irish people didn't make waiting at tables into an art form, moaning out a litany of char-grilled vegetables, dawn-picked mushrooms and stir-fried delicacies while the guests sat and listened. This was Dublin, where people liked to talk to each other. They hadn't lost the art of conversation so much that they expected to be entertained, instead, by a theatrical performance of the menu.

The thing was that he *is* proud of Ireland, and he talks about it all the time when he is not here. And people are great fun, quick on the uptake and seem to be having a good life for themselves. But they have this giant-sized chip on their shoulders which means that not a word can be said which is other than fulsome praise.

They cast you in a role: returned emigrant . . . back for the Christmas . . . you're meant to be gaping with awe about how marvellous everything is, faint at the size and scope of the new Financial Services Centre and not ask how much wealth it has generated for the country.

They want you to marvel over the Irish film industry and say that everywhere else the industry is finished. No films coming out of the States, Australia or France anymore. Ireland's your only man. He says just mildly that this is overstating the case a bit, and they all raise their eyes to heaven about him.

His mother gets upset and tries to take him aside. "Look at *The Sound of Music*. We loved that and that wasn't Irish," she says, and he wants to cry.

He has friends who have all taken up set dancing. He just remarked that when they were all at school and college they'd have died laughing at anyone doing Irish dancing – remember how they used to corpse themselves over a friend who put on a yellow or saffron skirt and long white socks. Remember?

It had fallen on deaf ears and lapsed memories. They didn't care to remember.

They were allowed to complain about things Irish, like the opening hours of the National Library, or the time of the last DART or the price of the pint or the freelance parking adviser who led you into spaces from which it would be impossible to emerge ever again. But *he* couldn't add his voice.

It pisses him off hugely to see people being so self-deluding and defensive. It's not as if he's saying there's anything really wrong with the place, but what kind of life is it if you've got to walk on eggshells for fear of offending people? What kind of homecoming is it if you can't be honest about your own home?

He was very disconsolate at the end of the holiday he had looked forward to for so long.

Had it ended well I wondered?

Not really. In fact, *not* well at all. You see the thing is, he was not playing the part of the successful guy coming back and telling people how things should be done. He had been four years over there, working very hard. Too hard in fact. There were many ways in which he would like to get a job back in Ireland, but not in an Ireland where you had to pretend it was the greatest country in the universe and you couldn't see its faults unless you wanted to be some kind of traitor in the camp.

There were ways in which he was softer and more sentimental than the rest of them. Take today, none of them came out to the airport to see him off. Now, when anyone came to his neck of the woods, they would drive miles, literally 100 miles to see someone off at the airport or to meet them.

But none of them stirred their stumps. And had he mentioned this? Well of course he had. He had said that for a country which prided itself so much on its so-called warmth and friendliness, it was unusual that they should ask him what time he wanted the taxi called. They had said that it was hard to park and there would be a lot of waiting around and surely it was better to say goodbye at home. And it was the last day before they went back to work so it didn't make sense . . .

He thought he was going to get some sympathy from me, but I told him how much we hated to hear anyone say our land wasn't all we hoped it to be. One of our own, gone for three or four years, was the one who had least permission to criticise. The hedgehog syndrome hides a fear that this *might* not be the best place on earth, and we don't want to be told about it in that destructive, chipping-away manner.

If he comes home next year, he should say that the place is fantastic and he doesn't know why he ever left. He should hint at a huge groundswell of emigrant envy for the way we all pulled the country together. All right, so it's not totally pure and honest . . . but then is every aspect of the 14-hour day he works over there as up front and sincere as he would like it to be?

AT THE END

"It has taken me a year to get the courage to write down his advice to those who want to do their best for friends who are about to die"

Years ago, there was a different code. You went to see a friend who was terminally ill and you looked into the eyes which would not see for much longer and you swore that the person had never looked better. You could see a terrific improvement since the last visit, and it would be no time at all before your friend was as right as rain again.

The more hearty and jovial the protestation, the better you thought the whole thing had gone. At least you felt you had handled the performance as it should have been done, and you were hugely relieved that nobody's guard had broken down and there had been no danger of anyone saying anything important about life and the leaving of it.

We don't know what they felt about it . . . the people who were at the receiving end of this histrionic pretence that everything was normal. It might have been some consolation to them, but surely they saw through it. In the dark hours of the night, they must have wondered why there was no communication left between friends who had once talked about everything.

Just when they needed real conversation most, they got reassurance, platitudes and, in fact, lies . . . and this from friends who used to sit up until dawn to discuss the meaning

159

of the Universe, the future of Art, and the likelihood of getting someone you fancied to fancy you.

Why should it turn to "Ho, ho, ho and aren't you looking well today"? It was because the well could not bear to admit the thought that the rest of the world was not well.

So what do you do if a friend is terminally ill? You do not want to go in with a face like the tombstone they know is not far away. You might not wish to bring up unaccustomed spiritual reading, likely aphorisms or new thinking on reincarnation.

Last year I had a friend who was given three months to live, and I asked him to tell me what were the best things people could do and what were the worst. He said that the very *worst* thing to do was to send a Get Well card, one with bunny rabbits crying into spotted handkerchiefs and saying "Sorry to hear you are not so well". He used to look at these cards blankly and knew that they were the conditioned response and automatic reflex of people who meant desperately well, but who had to hide behind totally inappropriate greeting cards.

He wanted to reply on another card, saying, "I'm trying, God damn it". But he didn't. And he didn't because he knew that the idiotic bits of card with hospital beds and sexy nurses and thermometers and bad puns hid the real message of sympathy and huge distress.

He said that he really didn't like people urging him to get another opinion and saying that it couldn't do any harm. It *would* do harm, he thought, because it would waste time, the one thing there wasn't much of left.

He preferred people to call it cancer if they spoke of it at all, rather than use some euphemism, and he also wished that he didn't have to spend so much time thanking people politely for their suggestions of healing crystals, prayers Never Known to Fail, or the laying-on of hands by someone who lived half a continent away.

Those of us who knew him well and asked him how he wanted to do it were told. He wanted to remember the good, laugh at the funny, hear all the gossip and try to be as normal as possible.

Even though he could no longer eat, he wanted to come to restaurants with us and didn't want to see anyone wince when he told the waiter he was on a diet.

He said that three months was a terrific bit of notice to get. You could make all kinds of arrangements, ask people to take a book from your collection, burn incriminating letters, heal old enmities, and send postcards to people you admired.

Once upon a time he had thought it would be good to die in his sleep or in a car crash. Something instantaneous. But there was a sense of time borrowed about this three-month sentence. Without being in the slightest maudlin, he said it was something we should all be lucky to get.

He said that he didn't really like bunches of flowers, there was too much of the sick room, and even the funeral parlour, about them arriving in great quantities. But what he really liked was a rake of stamped postcards or a couple of colourful tracksuits which he could wear around the house and a few videos to watch at night.

He didn't like letters telling him that lots of people had conquered this and surely he would too. But neither did he like the letters saying that he had a good innings and that, at 60, he had done everything. *He* wanted to be the judge of that.

But he did love to hear from the many people he had

known during his life, saying briefly that they had heard about his diagnosis and that they were sorry. Letters that then went on to say things he could hold on to, things about time well spent, marvellous places seen, and memories that would live forever. All this brought a smile to his face and made the tapestry richer and less laced with regret.

He said that, if at all possible, he would like there to be no tears, but he knew this was hard, and he didn't mind unnaturally bright eyes, because he knew this was a sign of grief felt but bravely fought back. He could understand why some people hadn't the guts to come and see him, but he wished they had.

It has taken me a year to get the courage to write down his advice to those who want to do their best for friends who are about to die. A year in which I have never ceased to admire his bravery and honesty and to believe that there may be a lot of it around if we could recognise it.

We planted a rose tree, a Super Star, in his memory, and at last I feel the strength to pass on his advice to those who might learn from it.

LESS IS MORE

"I advise a lot of people to do less, not more, next year"

All right, so Margaret Thatcher got up at five o'clock in the morning but did it do her all that much good? Joan Collins has slaved to look young, but must she not get tired of people looking at her ears for signs of scars from a face-lift, rather than into her eyes, when she's talking to them? Does Rupert Murdoch wake each day and say "Oh goody I'm delighted that I made a resolution to buy up every newspaper I saw"?

Do the men and women in the money houses see the New Year as a spreadsheet of some sort, where numbers and figures dance ahead of them like some kind of Pied Piper? Do the dieters see the year ahead as a hand-to-hand struggle against the demon god Excess? Do the excessively house-proud see it as a year when every centimetre of wood that can be seen, should be stripped down and begun all over again?

I have heard the resolutions all around me. They all involve doing more, working harder, putting in longer hours, concentrating fully, being stern with themselves.

It doesn't matter that it won't happen, that it's all a dream really . . . this is not the point. The point is that it just seems too much, too puritan, too pessimistic. Too much belief that we are, in fact, all rats and that the race has begun. To stand still or to pause for a moment would mean being trampled on by the other rats, the eager, winning rats. To say that things aren't too bad as they are, and let's enjoy them, is to lose ground. On, on, more, more . . .

I advise a lot of people to do less, not more, next year. It's not a sign of inertia, smugness, complacency and the imminent end of civilisation if we are just happy with what we have, rather than forever seeking to increase it.

Why should my American friend resolve to do yet another night course in business administration so that she'll make senior vice-president of the company before she's 50? Why should she do this? Why deny herself a life, friends, love, time just sitting at home, resting?

Yes, I know it's great to get somewhere, to be recognised, but in her case, what will it mean? Most of her colleagues will hate her; some will be pleased, but jealous; her family will be proud, but know that now they'll never see her; people like myself will be bewildered and won't know what kind of an honour it is and why it was worth it, but will be sorry that it means she will never take a vacation again.

Why should this man I know make a resolution that he'll get a proper loan and expand his small business which is doing perfectly well? None of his children wants to go into it with him. He employs four people. If things work out the way he hopes, he'll have a staff of 14 . . . and a bank loan like a thundercloud for the foreseeable future. He's 54; he doesn't want to be a Michael Smurfit. Does he want to be listening to the market reports from Hong Kong and Tokyo at the crack of dawn? Does he want to be angst-ridden about budgets instead of just complaining about drink and cigarettes? Does he think he'll be a better person?

When will he spend the money he earns? There won't be time to go abroad on a holiday, or peace and ease to sit and enjoy a nicer house and garden. Will his wife be glad to have a designer outfit, but no nice, easy-going man around the place of an evening, who might go and walk the dog with her, or take a drive out to look at the sea?

Tell me about this girl who is 20 and doesn't have a boyfriend. Now I'm not on some kind of crusade to keep the world fat or anything, but honestly, she's nine stone, she's lovely, but she thinks if she were seven stone it would all happen for her. So the plan is that, tomorrow, she will go on an 800 calorie a day diet.

It's a pity it's a Saturday, she says, but, then if you leave it till Monday, it's a show of weakness, isn't it? And it's even more of a pity because there are two parties on this weekend and she won't be able to eat any sausages or anything. She often feels a bit self-conscious. People will look at her and say to themselves "Look at that big fat girl there on a diet; not doing her much good from the signs of it".

Wouldn't it be great if someone could tell her that maybe if she lost just a few pounds, for the pride of it, and put a smile on her face, she might enjoy the year, and even enjoy it in company?

Surely after Christmas, when so many plans were thought of and abandoned, so many resolutions made and broken about having everything ready in time, about not getting red-faced and fussed, about not snapping the heads off immediate family while smiling graciously at strangers . . . surely we noticed that the skies don't fall on us if we don't keep to a plan? And that Christmas was fine really when we were the way we were?

I don't think that it would be holding back the march of a nation, or the interests of progress, to say that too many of us grit our teeth and try to work out a totally different Spartan, energetic, workaholic regime for ourselves, instead of facing another year with gratitude and relief.

Those of us who have a house to live in, a job to earn a living from, our health to be able to enjoy pain-free days and night, should not be attacked if we say "isn't this fine? Aren't we grand as we are?"

The point might be – like the world-class golfer who said that he would never forget to enjoy the game, smell the grass and see the flowers – that maybe we should resolve to be happy rather than perfect, peaceful rather than stretching to achieve. We should begin another year with hope and confidence, rather than the self-imposed gloom of so many would-be superpeople.

This time next year we might be saying that it was the best year of all, the year of living uncompetitively . . . the year we counted the blessings we had rather than chased after dreams.

PART IV

IN THE PUBLIC DOMAIN

BISHOP'S MOVE

"If Eamonn Casey came back and faced everything and raised a quarter of a million pounds for it, that would really be paying his dues"

It's no use talking about what he should or shouldn't have done in the past. The past is over. What should he do today? I think he should get on a plane and come home from wherever he is. He won't have to call a press conference because it will be known that he's coming, and there will be plenty of people waiting. Then he should say very simply that he was sorry for running away and that he's back now, he'd like a job somewhere in some parish but not for the next three weeks. He should explain that for the next three weeks he will be very busy indeed. Writing his own book. There are very many publishers who have desk-top publishing and could have the book out in no time. It would be announced from the word go that all the royalties would go to Trocaire.

He should not listen to anyone who says that it's more *dignified* to stay away. There is little dignity in being an exile from your own country when everyone is reading and tutting over your escapades. What extra dignity do you get by not being there to avoid their eyes?

None.

People are not going to forget him because he's not here. On the contrary. They are going to be talking about him anyway when Annie Murphy's book is published, even more than they talked about him last May, if that were possible.

But if he's not here, he's even fairer game to tut-tut over than if he were seen to have the courage to come back and face it.

Eamonn Casey would do well to remember two people at this time; they are John Profumo and Ben Dunne. You don't hear many people attacking either of those lads today.

When Profumo is mentioned, people remember that he stood his ground, did social work in the East End of London, craved no publicity, and behaved with extreme dignity. Ben Dunne behaved like a big innocent child who was caught with his hand in the cookie jar. He said he was desperately sorry, he had made an eejit out of himself and he wouldn't do it again.

Fair enough. Those were the words you heard every time Ben Dunne's name was mentioned thereafter. Fair enough, or fair dues to him. The facing of it was bigger than the doing of it, and the second seemed to wipe out the first.

Now both John Profumo and Ben Dunne had a wife each to help them. And things being as they are in the clerical celibacy business, Eamonn Casey does not, which makes him all alone. He must rely on people whom he trusts are out for his good.

A lot of these people are those who believe that the less said the better, and that it will all be forgotten and become yesterday's news, if no further fuel is added. This could be the well-meaning and sincere, cautious advice of those who truly think that it's a nine day wonder and will blow away.

But Eamonn Casey was always a showman, a larger-than-life person who was not known for treading the cautious path. When other bishops would wonder about the gravitas of singing a song on the *Late Late Show*, he was able to sing one, or tell a joke or laugh like a big jolly friar of old, and people loved him for it.

He shouldn't heed those who say that coming home would give scandal. To whom would it give scandal? There can hardly be anyone over three years of age who doesn't know about it already.

What started as a private affair has become a public one and it doesn't do a bit of good for his friends to whinge about this and say it's his own business and encourage him to be an ostrich. He has a couple of decades left: why spend them in hiding from people who would definitely forgive him if he played it straight, from people who would say fair enough, and, particularly, from his own son?

The best thing, surely, for that boy would be to hear his father say publicly that it was an era of huge confusion and hypocrisy and that he hoped and prayed that the years to come will not be so small-minded. If he were to say to Peter Murphy that he was sorry for denying him all those years, then the boy might well have the *big* heart to think that his father had been punished enough, and to accept what he had to give now.

And because of the way things turned out, he will not need to give Peter any money. Peter's mother's book has organised that for him. So he can give all the money to a charity that suffered very much and very unfairly because of him. Nobody ever said that Trocaire was to blame for what happened, nor that it wasn't doing great work, but somehow people hadn't the heart to support it, in the way they used to, for a few months after the story first broke. If Eamonn Casey came back and faced everything and raised a quarter of a million pounds for it, that would really be paying his dues.

To do this he would have to write a really spectacular book that people would want to read.

It couldn't be a Holy Joe job, not a list of vague regrets about being unworthy, nor a smiting of his breast about being a sinner. There are no sales in that. It couldn't be a self-justification book – that really *would* be undignified. Nor could it be full of denial or nit-picking – it wasn't Thursday it was Friday, it wasn't this number of times it was that number of times – no repeat of Adam's poor script in the Garden of Eden about it being the Woman who made me do it.

Nor should he run her down, say she was like a sack of potatoes in bed, that she was loopy. In her book, it is understood that she says all the time how much she loved him.

Maybe he should say how much he loved her, if he did. He could write of the expectations people have of their clergy and whether these are realistic or not. Or about the whole celibacy argument: would priests be better, stronger men if they were allowed to share a life and love with a mate? He could tell of the effect Annie had on him, the wish to see his child grow up, which was almost stifled by the fear that anyone should know the child existed.

Bishop Casey could always tell a good story and tell it well. The main thing he must do is tell this one quickly – while there is still money to be made from his side of things, money that can be spent doing good.

And, if he wants to test the water, he could try it out in a newspaper interview, prove that there is no virtue in this so-called dignity of silence.

This paper has treated him honourably. He knows the telephone number.

(We'll never know how things might stand now for Eamonn Casey had he followed my advice immediately, and to the letter.

As it turned out, Annie Murphy's book didn't do him anything like the insurmountable damage some people feared, and lots of others began calling for his return, including the Archbishop of Tuam who said he'd dearly love to see Bishop Casey come home.

But the Bishop delayed and then began making forays back, gave a couple of lengthy interviews, signed some autographs in Florida where he arrived for the World Cup, and his brothers in the hierarchy are taking a somewhat different line. They're complaining about his excessively high profile and the wisdom of his wearing his Episcopal attire on the altar in Cork. The Archbishop of Dublin observed in August of 1994 that these sporadic appearances seemed simply to "tear open the wounds again".

Trocaire soldiers on through famines and wars.)

ON THE LINE

"The land he wants to rule is a talkative land, where people value their conversations and do not like them cut short"

If he were to analyse the poison in the chalice, Brian Cowen would probably find that the most dangerous section is the statistics. There is no way that anyone in this country believes that 72 per cent of local calls are of less than three minutes' duration. When Brian had to respond to the rebalancing tariff proposals presented to him by Telecom, he knew he would have to wear a flak jacket. If you are in cabinet, presumably you can't say that you don't want to be associated with something that is going to draw the fire of every consumer group in the country, but Brian should have refused that particular figure. He must know that, unless you live in a world where people bark "Buy or Sell" down phones, conversations go on much longer.

And it's not too late. He could say that new information has come to his attention and that in the light of this . . . and that would be true. He would be quite truthful in saying this because the man must be deafened with the sounds of disbelief. None of us will accept the assurances that it has all been measured scientifically. There are some things that will never be believed.

I am in a fairly good position to report on this since I listen to a great many crossed lines. These people do not hang up in three minutes. They go on and on and on. They tell each other about the everyday business of living. They tell of housework and hangovers and heartbreak and harassment at work. And these are not just the famous teenagers who are meant to be the only ones who want to yak on for hours. They are friends relaxing after a day's work, they are sisters talking about their families, they are colleagues talking about new schemes at work, they are golfers re-living every hole. They are people who are going to make a pudding who want advice on the recipe, they are tellers of interminable tales about traffic jams or trains that were late. It is to our everlasting credit as a nation that we are never short of a word.

Who are these snappish people who get onto a phone and are off it again before they have time to say anything more than a greeting? They do not exist, and Brian Cowen, who is a man with the words "leadership material" written in the pupils of both eyes, should question these three-minute myths.

And suppose there are some short conversations in your life, like ringing a bank or an organisation. By the time you have sung along with *Alas my Love you do me wrong* from the Greensleeves tape, or the singularly inappropriate *Where the Deer and the Antelope Play* that I get when I ring a place where the clouds are pretty threatening all day, then your three minutes are often up before you get connected.

Brian Cowen has been told about the old and the lonely. He has been at pains to say that these were not his target and I'm sure he is truthful in this. After all even if you didn't have "leadership material" tattooed on your chest, you wouldn't be likely to say that you were setting out to penalise the old and the lonely. It would not be a good career move.

But if he paused to think, he would realise that the old and the lonely are not a market segment who will want to hang up after three minutes. I am not very old and lonely yet, but when I am, if I get there, I would like to think that there was time to ramble on a bit without people thinking what a pathetic spendthrift lonely old fool I was. I don't want to feel I have to return everyone's calls saying that I would prefer to initiate them myself and be in charge of the duration in case I wasted anyone's money. I don't want to hear warning pings when I am coming to the end of my allotted time of chat.

Did Brian ask for proof that 72 per cent of people hung up in under three minutes? If I were in his position I wouldn't have opened my little beak until I had been shown the machinery that recorded it, and checked it out for myself. Perhaps, in his world, people bark staccato ministerial things at each other and hang up. I doubt it though. And anyway politicians are meant to have an understanding about the way we live. He must have noticed the way people talk, he must have seen enough of it to demand that the statistics be double-checked.

The telephone used to be a luxury, people will tell you, wagging metaphorical fingers. I don't like that line. It is so patronising to tell people that they should be grateful for a development in communications, and be prepared to get off the phone before they have got on, just because it's far from telephones many of the previous generation were reared. The telephone is a comfort and a friend. A caring society should ensure that it remains so at some acceptable cost, without all this preaching and pontificating and telling us to be grateful that long-distance deals can now be done more cheaply from the Financial Services Centre.

Brian hasn't told us all to get up and get cracking before eight which is probably another sensible career move. The number of people who would like to be lifted from the bed for a pleasant aimless chat at seven is a limited one. Then at night people are often tired and busy or are with friends or watching television.

I could tell him a heap of stories. An old man phones his daughter at lunch-time. She has the phone in the kitchen, she chops and peels and cleans as she talks. He is on for about half an hour. It's great. It won't be any more.

A widow is worried about money. She drives her children mad by saying "this is costing a fortune". About a year ago they got her off that, they told her proudly that local call charges were not related to time. Not any more. A kind woman keeps in touch with a proud neighbour by ringing her each day and discussing the bridge problem in *The Irish Times*. It's only kindness really, an excuse to keep in touch. But from now on it would smack of charity.

I am leaving out the life and death phone calls because it is assumed that the endless good and helpful Samaritans and other helplines will be looked after.

I am really asking Brian Cowen to find who these short-callers are, the folks who are gone before you know they are there. If they exist, then it will be such an interesting piece of research. If they don't, he can be magnanimous and say that he decided to look into it. After all there is a precedent in Fianna Fáil. De Valera was known to look into his heart about things and didn't suffer for it. The leadership lights in Minister Cowen's eyes could well turn out to be in brightest neon if he plays this one properly. If he remembers that the land he wants to rule is a talkative land where people value their conversations and do not like them cut short by any rebalancing tariff proposals whatsoever.

(Mr Cowen did not talk much about figures or phones in his latter days as minister. This could be because business people who make a lot of long-distance phone calls do seem to be doing better on the bills, of course, and also because Telecom Eireann made a profit of £81 million last year).

SCREENSTRUCK

"Michael D Higgins always says that he prides himself on doing things quickly"

It doesn't matter if it goes off half cock; the main thing is that it gets started. People's memories are short. Soon the great triumphant picture of Neil Jordan standing there holding the Oscar will fade or just be crowded out by pictures of other people holding their awards. The iron doesn't stay hot forever.

The main thing is to get everyone into a lather of

excitement about it, to let there be a huge amount of hope where once there was a blank wall. There shouldn't be months of deliberation about how it is to be composed and what voice it will speak with. There's no point in getting the Row started and the Split organised before it's appointed.

The bad news has been that, since 1987, there has been nowhere that could act as a kind of focus, a channel for the dreams and plans of Irish film-makers. The good news is that there will be one again. It would be a great pity to waste endless hours wondering and speculating about its composition. It should meet next week.

You see there's no way it's going to please everyone. It can't possibly do that. The main thing is to make it wide-ranging and give it a lot of money. And then the legitimate long-running complaint, that our country doesn't give a damn about one of the main art and entertainment forms of our day, can be stilled. For a while. It can be replaced, of course, with many equally legitimate complaints about the people who are running it. The lot they let in, the lot they excluded and whether it knows any part of itself from its elbow in terms of making films.

At least it will be *there*, and all the talented Irish people who have had to fight to work in film industries outside this country will be able to fight with it and challenge it and picket it and denounce it. But there will be something there to acknowledge the huge impact of Irish people in the film industry all over the world.

When I was roaming around the planet for four months I was not moving at all in film circles, but in every place I went they were talking about Irish films.

Many people knew about Ireland only through their visits to the cinema or the video rental shop: they thought there must be a great dynamism about the place and said that the government was very enlightened to promote it so much. Loyalty to my own country and rage with the political party that had killed the Film Board warred within me, and I used to say that it was all done very much against the odds. They had to find finance from the trees.

This caused a lot of head-shaking. They thought it was like the palmy days of Gough Whitlam, when suddenly the world knew about Australia through a series of glorious Australian films. Now, not every Australian liked things like *Sunday Too Far Away*, full of grog-obsessed sheep shearers. It gave a down-market impression of the place, they said. But it also showed a world of enthusiasm, colour, light and love that made people begin to understand the many sides of their country.

It wasn't paid for by the Australian Tourist Board, any more than the marvellous *Commitments* was financed by Bórd Fáilte, but that's not the point. A film industry is not a propaganda wing of the government. There were a lot of people who thought the Abbey Theatre shouldn't produce plays set in Dublin slums, where drink and violence were accepted as the norm. And fortunately nobody took that kind of view seriously enough to bypass O'Casey.

Of course, the Film Board will not have an easy road. We'll all think our projects are being passed over because they're too serious, too popular, too intellectual or too down-market.

There will not be a person in the country who has written a book or even hatched an idea who will not believe that, if that shower were out and proper reasonable people in, then it would all be perfect.

There will be those who will want to judge it by its

commercial success, others by its artistic merit. Some by the box office, some by the film festival awards.

We don't get any wiser by speculating and coming up with one format after another. There is no Dream Team. It may be better to have real practitioners, people who know how to do it and have done it with success, on the Film Board. Then is there a fear that they would want to allot all the money to themselves and their friends?

And are they right? Maybe they *are* the people who should have the funds instead of a crowd of amateurs with big notions and no talent.

But this is a problem that has never been solved. Should there be hoteliers on the board of Bórd Fáilte, or even as its chairmen? Wouldn't that mean an unfair advantage for that person's hotels? But then, if you have people who don't know one end of a hotel from another, isn't that equally cracked?

Bórd Fáilte didn't break up in disarray; the problem was addressed in a different way. But the really stupid thing would have been to have had no Bórd Fáilte, no tourist office to let people know about our land.

Michael D Higgins always says that he prides himself on doing things quickly. I'm sure he'll do this one very quickly altogether. I bet we'll all be reading and disagreeing with his choice on Monday morning over breakfast.

(*Michael D proved very amenable to suggestions and moved at the speed of fast forward, and as a result Bórd Scannáin na hEireann is one of the great success stories of our times. Financial investment in Irish films in 1993 and 1994 soared to £29 million, compared to £11.5 million in the previous six years, and at the last count 30 films were either completed, underway or on schedule for those two years.*)

GAMBLERS ANONYMOUS

*"People thought the Names were like benevolent despots who left
their money there in case the Titanic sank again"*

So there are over 300 Irish Names in Lloyds. And they may
be in financial difficulty. Why is it so hard to be
sympathetic? I mean, you'd be a little sorry for some halfwit
who lost his salary on a horse that was not as fleet of foot as
had been hoped. You'd have a bit of pity for the fools flung
over machines in Las Vegas, and the card-players with
dulled eyes trying to fill a straight yet again. Why is it hard
to feel anything for the Names?

Possibly because, with a few exceptions, they are not
Names at all; they are Anons. There was a meeting of Irish
Names a while back, and they were all rushing out of the
door of the hotel with newspapers over their heads and their
faces stuck under the armpits of their coats in case anyone
would know who they were. Lord Mountcharles, Lord
Killanin and Dr Edmond O'Flaherty have always "outed"
themselves about being Names and it was assumed that most
Irish business people, who can lay their hands easily on a
quarter of a million so that they can afford to "sort of let it
lie there", are in Lloyds. But it was as secret as the Masons
and the Knights, with an added aura of incredible financial
rectitude.

A Name was a person who Kept Things Going. And they
did very nicely out of it. The point about being a Name was
that you had to tell Lloyds you had £250,000 which they
could call on if needs be.

You had to do more than tell them, I imagine – I think you had to show it to them.

But the great advantage was you didn't have to give it to them: you could invest it in something else and every year you got your interest on that investment. And, because Lloyds knew that your money was always there to call on if ever they needed it, they paid you as well. Around 10 per cent. So it worked out that you got about £25,000 a year from them as well as what you got from your deposit account or whatever it was.

It was nice work being a Name. It was, of course, perfectly legal. More than legal: people thought that Names were like benevolent despots who left their money there in case the Titanic sank again.

And, as the years went on, the Names must have been excused for thinking that this was money for old rope – every year the interest came in on their investments as usual, and every year there was the nice little earner from Lloyds. And I am absolutely certain that many Names did very good things with their money: I don't see them all as bad barons twirling their moustaches and grinding the poor ever further into the ground.

But if a Name had two brain cells to rub together then, somewhere along the line, it must have crossed his happy mind that there was some risk involved in this.

Ever since the confused aristocracy babbled their way to the guillotine, there can't have been anyone who believed that there was some kind of system which allowed the rich to get richer with no risk until the end of time. They *must* have said, even in the privacy of the boudoir, that this caper was too good to be true. Surely a cliché about the bubble being bound to burst might have slid into the subconscious?

But I have never known such bellyaching among Names, and Friends of Names. There are accusations of Insider Trading, Double Dealing, People in the Know, a Golden Circle which steered newcomers into dangerous areas and let them become involved in potential powder kegs – such as the US environmental lobby and all the upcoming claims because of asbestos policies.

If there is an Inner Circle, and it has been in no way proved . . . so what? You don't hear anyone being outraged on behalf of the eejit who lost his money because he hadn't as much info about the state of mind and the state of fetlock of some horse. The only thing I see to praise in those who gamble heavily at the races and the card tables is that they *know* they are gambling.

What kind of brain-fade made the Names unaware of this?

People who suspect that horses are held back and that decks are rigged still put their money at risk. Those who know that the bank must win in a casino still lay their counters on the red and the black. Anyone with stocks and shares knows they can go up or down.

Why did the Names stand alone in the commercial world and not understand that some day this capital they had pledged might be called in? Lloyds is very old-fashioned; therein lay a lot of its charm. It's full of ponderous old-chap tradition, and manages to preserve, amid the new architecture and high technology of the City of London, a sort of superior let's-not-be-vulgar-and-talk-about-trade-and-money-or-anything-sordid atmosphere.

It's nearly 200 years since a ship wrecked on the Zuider Zee; it was called *HMS Lutine*. Everyone in Lloyds was nearly wiped out over that one, and the sum was half a million. Years later they found its plunder and made it into a chair for Lloyds' Chairmen, and they hung up its bell – which was rung once when a shipwreck was reported and rung twice when a ship was overdue. That was fairly mind-blowing as well.

Last week in a restaurant in Dublin, I heard a group of diners sympathising with a Name. You would have thought that he been made redundant through no fault of own. You would have believed that his hard-worked-for earnings had been abstracted by a crooked accountant. You would have thought that a conman had sold him a property that did not exist.

But no, all that had happened to him was that he had gambled. And the Lutine bell began ringing for almost £3 billion. And he had to pay his share.

I was longing to tell them not to cry for him. That other people have had to move to smaller houses and live a very different lifestyle. But I wouldn't interrupt their dinner. And anyway, I could tell them today.

(Some Names have banded together and are taking all kinds of legal action in the British courts alleging malpractice, negligence and other dire practices on the part of the enterprises they were persuaded to underwrite. Other Names have just gone down the tubes. Lloyds of London is still going strong. The chaps wouldn't let a bit of unpleasantness set the old institution back.)

QUEEN'S MOVE

*"Unlike the rest of the team . . . she gives good value
for her civil list payment"*

If I were an old friend of the Queen Mother I would come
and have a nice gin with her this weekend and suggest quite
seriously that she take over the throne.

Her daughter, the present Queen of England, is having a
bad time: she has begun to talk in Latin, she is aching to
retire and can't because all her children have gone off the
rails and the grandchildren are too young.

Who would be a more suitable person to put on the
throne than her mother? The only Royal not to have been
toppled from the pedestals of yesteryear, the only one who
knows that the main qualification for being a Royal at all is
to smile constantly and pretend you are having a great time
everywhere.

There is another advantage about the Queen Mother
taking over. At the age of 94, her life-expectancy would not
be enormous and even the most dedicated anti-monarchist
could hardly object to her serving her term.

And then, in the fullness of time when she is about 100,
and the new millennium dawns, the monarchy could come
to a gracious and logical end without any revolution, and
there could be a glut of nostalgic books about how wonderful
they all were in their time.

The Queen Mother has a nice soothing aura about her. I
have seen her at the races presenting cups and talking to
trainers and discussing the water jump with jockeys as if she

might be saddling up herself a bit later in the afternoon. The older she gets, the more pastel her clothes become and the more feathers and fringes appear in her hats. She is like a marvellous mad bird of paradise in any crowd, her hand raised in automatic wave position, her smile wider and wider, her corgis growling contentedly at her feet, and a look of great regret when she has to leave whatever housing estate, memorial ceremony, shipyard or sports event that they have wheeled her out to that day. Unlike the rest of the team – who seem to be pawing at the ground, looking over their shoulders and sighing – she gives good value for her civil list payment.

She is a loved old-fashioned relic of a time gone by. And so, in many ways, is the monarchy itself. If they were united in one person, it would be a spectacular way to draw it all to a close.

Look at all the crises that would be solved at one swoop. The present Queen, who seems to have a very sincere sense of duty about the whole thing, would feel secure if she let her mother take over. It would end all this angst about whether Di can be crowned or not, or whether it should skip Charles and go to the little prince. You get the feeling that she is hanging on in there until the little prince becomes a big enough prince to take over.

But if she were to look *not* to far-distant generations but instead look back one, she has the perfect candidate waiting in the wings.

Presumably the Queen Mother wouldn't be having embarrassing conversations on mobile phones. She wouldn't give rise to endless speculation like the next lot down the line do, making the British public ask seriously in pubs and in acres of print: Are They Worth It? or Is Their Day Over?

If the Queen Mother were to be crowned with the tacit – or maybe even formal – agreement that she were to be the last of the line, then it would mean that Charles could marry Camilla, which he really should do fairly smartish anyway. Not just because it's the only honourable and gentlemanly sort of thing to do if a lady's name has been mentioned and rather more than mentioned, but because Camilla is taking on all the appearances of a very loose cannon indeed on the deck. I have seen photographs of her glaring at things in general that would unhinge me if I were Charles. And if one's grandmother were safely crowned and anointed and there were no question of one having to stand in readiness for it, one could get on with doing The Right Thing.

And those little boys could have a normal life if they didn't have to think about shouldering responsibilities and taking over a job that Daddy should have done and didn't, and in general having to sort out the mess that Mummy and Daddy and all the silly uncles and aunties got them into. What a huge relief to them it would be to see Great-Grandmother smiling away with a crown on over her hat, and Grandma looking happy out with her corgis in the rain while Grandfather growled and shot small birds all day. The whole scheme has so much to recommend it the Queen Mother would be surprised that she hadn't thought of it before.

But – and it's always wise, when giving advice, to anticipate the argument – but, she might say, perhaps it would be an imposition, maybe they mightn't like an elderly relative moving in on them all and taking things over?

This is where I would lean over confidentially and say: So what?

They all purport to take this monarchy business seriously

but the Queen Mother is the only one who actually went out and worked at it. She was never expecting it; the others were born to it or married into it or discovered that they were stuck with it at an early age. But the Queen Mother thought she was marrying a nice younger son, a duke certainly, but had not a notion of his turning into a king until all that Bad Behaviour back in the 1930s when Edward went off course.

And she stuck to it all, helping a nervous man with a speech impediment make broadcasts to the nation – which frightened him to death – and she was always there smiling through air raids and more and more impossible weddings. They even brought her to Scotland to give a bit of respectability to Anne's second wedding and what thanks does she get for it?

None at all.

Normally I wouldn't inflame a friend against the family, I see my role more as soother of ruffled feelings and patter-down of possible rows.

But honestly. The woman is 93. She choked and was taken to hospital. You couldn't get into the place with all the flowers from well-wishers. But did her family come to see her? No, they did not.

She has two daughters, six grandchildren. And for three days the news bulletins of the BBC led with a health report on her. And then it dawned on some clouded PR brain that common people go to see their relatives in hospital and the Duke of York was rustled up for a photocall.

I'd say to the Queen Mother, don't waste any time worrying about their sensitivities, they seem to have lost them.

And then we would plan what we'd both wear for the Coronation.

ROAD TO ROME

"The whole dangerous business of bells and smells"

When Katherine Worseley married the Duke of Kent in 1961, she was a nice ladylike girl from an upper-class family in Yorkshire and there was a sigh of relief because she was good-looking, quiet and she wasn't a Catholic.

That was over 30 years ago when a great many real people still thought it was terribly important that the monarchy shouldn't be tied to Rome's apron strings with overtones of Armadas and Counter-Reformations, and the whole dangerous business of bells and smells. Life was complicated then for royalists, because the tragic fact was that the only suitable spouses for the Windsors and their cousins seemed to be – perish the thought – Catholic monarchies. There were dozens of likely starters in the crumbling palaces of Europe, whose lineage was fine and royal but who dug with the wrong foot.

Nowadays surely it couldn't matter less, or so you might think. Normal people would be forgiven for thinking that the British royal family has given such unwilling entertainment over the last few years, in so many spheres, that the mere conversion to Catholicism of a woman who is married to someone 18th in line to the throne should pass without comment. But they would be wrong. It has been analysed and argued down to the bone: it has been made into a drama, a threat, a straw in the wind. They say it has all to do with the Church of England's confusion over the ordination of women priests. They say the floodgates are about to open and that hordes of upper-crust Anglicans are about to defect. They don't see a tired, pleasant, quiet woman who obviously seriously thinks that her way to God is clearer and more satisfying through membership of the Catholic Church. They have turned the whole thing into a circus.

I have great sympathy for the Duchess of Kent. With over half her lifetime lived in a goldfish bowl, she couldn't even have a miscarriage or a depression in private. When she agreed to be a patron of the Samaritans, she also wanted to work with them as a sympathetic listening voice on the phone. But then, when it leaked out that Samaritan Katie was really her Royal Highness, it changed everything. She was in the limelight when her son married what was thought to be an unsuitable bride. Canadian, Catholic, divorced. Then her other son was caught with a teeny bit of cannabis – the first royal drugs bust. Everything she did, or her family did, was a matter for public attention.

The tabloids said alternately that she was caring or unstable, depending on how they felt about her. She felt human sympathy and sorrow for the Czech tennis player, Jana Novotna, who burst into tears in front of everyone at Wimbledon. She hugged the girl with the kind of response that most of us would think was good, rather than staring frostily past her and pretending it wasn't happening, like many other royals would have done. But the tabloids blew it all up to the skies; either she was as caring as Mother Teresa, a totally inappropriate comparison, or she was definitely unstable, her own tears never being far from the surface. At least Katherine Worseley's husband, who is Grand Master of Britain's Freemasons, would have the huge advantage of secrecy on his side.

She was always a religious Anglican and, as many felt before her, she must have felt that she could take a further step and moved from her high church practice of the Protestant faith to joining the Church of Rome. At the same time as she was making that decision, there were also Catholics who left the Church of Rome because they disapproved of some Papal teachings. All these are people of good faith and honour, following their consciences. All over the world, people are finding personal roads to Damascus, seeing salvation, seeing a better way to live or a hope and a promise by taking a different route. In general, people wish them well and they get on with it. But then they are not duchesses. Katherine Worseley isn't allowed to get on with it.

Among the upper-class Catholics in England there is a triumphalism that is as irritating as the frightened braying of those who regard the conversion as a defection. The Brompton Oratory set, the Farm Street set, the Saint Ethelreda or Hatton Garden set all hope that the Duchess will be part of their lot.

All the various Catholic charities are clamouring to have her name on their notepaper; there is a feeling of having arrived, being accepted, given a belated pat on the back for being part of a tribe once in the wilderness but now acceptable to royal duchesses. Not one bit of this is the Duchess of Kent's fault. She was quiet and unobtrusive about it all. She asked Queen Elizabeth's permission quietly in advance because she didn't want the Niagara Falls of a reaction if she did it off her own bat. She couldn't become a secret Catholic; that's not how to do things if she had the courage and the faith to want to join openly. The early Christians, who hid their faith rather than be eaten by lions, weren't considered much of an advertisement for their religion. But it has become a huge political football. People are very busy attributing motives to her that she may never have had. It's her anti-abortion stance that made her take the final leap, they say. It's a protest about the way society in general, and the royal family in particular, have been behaving. It's giving Queen Elizabeth the opportunity to show how private faith and the established Church of England do not have to go hand in hand. It's part of the slow process to disestablish the Church of England and allow Charles, as a divorced man, to be crowned king.

There are growlings, too, among many ordinary British Catholics; why did she have to have a cardinal do the receiving into the Church bit? Wouldn't an ordinary priest have done? I don't find a great difficulty with that. If you accept that it is a class-dominated society, and that she's in the top drawer and that he is a prince of the church, it is probably the correct diplomatic procedure. Anyway, she knows him and he is a friend and he's not out looking for more limelight at this stage in his life. What I do object to is the way everyone is reading so much into it on a political, social and tribal level. We have to assume that these people read some of the papers some of the time. I'd like to think that she might find peace and hope, and would wish that for anyone who makes a decision based on faith. I hope that she will be able to ignore all the ballyhoo, and stories of the Gunpowder Plot, and rumours of her being a Pied Piper about to lead all the other confused members of the royal family on the road to Rome.

HORSE LAUGH

"Stewards with Attitude have run things for far too long"

The ludicrous and upsetting farce when the Grand National did not start at Aintree might have some good results if the control of the whole thing can be finally wrested from all these pompous, self-important people in hats who prance around, delighted with themselves, until something happens and then fall apart like broken biscuits.

Racing, which is meant to be democratic, a good day out for all, a sport enjoyed by rich and poor, is in fact nothing of the sort. There is a class structure in racing which would make the hair stand up on your head if you were to think about it. From the gear they wear to the price of tickets to the various enclosures, from the different bars for different drinks to the railed-off areas for royalty over there, and corporate entertaining over here, how can anyone think it's an egalitarian outing?

There was a time within recent memory when divorced people couldn't go into the Royal Enclosure at Ascot. Admittedly that was before such a ruling would exclude almost the entire royal family, but this was an example of the pretentious and repressive legislation that those who ran racing were able to get away with.

Stewards with Attitude have run things for far too long. Last week their cover was blown and it's time for the people who actually do give the public what they want to take over their own sport.

God knows I'm not an enthusiastic gambler, as the State

of Nevada could tell you – it didn't lose serious money until I went to Las Vegas and drank the drink and watched the lavish spectacles without consigning anything significant to the slot machines or blackjack tables. But I have *been* to the races in all kinds of places and I've enjoyed them in spite of bullying-looking people with badges and bowlers and serious sense-of-humour failure.

The guys who are meant to run things are the only people who appear to be having no fun at all at the races. They have a particular gesture. It's an outstretched arm and a pointing finger, a bit like generals. They move in twos and threes, pointing, hissing, frowning. They seem to know everything and disapprove of most of it. When races *do* start, which is most of the time, they sort of glower after the departing horses as if they were letting the place down.

When races *don't* start, like last Saturday, they turn ashen white and start pointing and gesturing and opening rule books and shouting and reading out rules to people in the aggrieved tones of tyrannical schoolmasters who can't believe that the Lower Fourth are a crowd of dunderheads. Then they go into conclave and come out shouting a totally different decision from the one they had pointed out previously with such pained and speaking-to-slow-learner delivery.

This is a deeply silly class of person and should not be in charge for much longer.

Even those of us who had only put a pound each way on Kildimo for the sociability of it all, who had come in, drawn the curtains against the bright April sunlight and sat down to watch the race, could see that we were watching the dying whimper of a breed that will be less credible than any of the strange dinosaurs recreated for us these days.

Gesturing and arrogant, they were unable to admit that

anything had, or could possibly have, gone wrong. Later they searched like mad for a scapegoat in the form of a man with a flag, a figure who seemed to step straight out of the past – when he would have run in front of the horseless carriages to give the news that a machine was in the road.

Maybe it needed that shambles to show what a pathetic set-up it all was. But it was a hard price to have to pay. I found myself in tears with John White and, in the usual fit of parallelism I get about almost every aspect or life, I thought myself into the position of being bent over the neck of Esha Ness and going ba-doom ba-doom ba-doom past the winning post, saying to myself won't Jenny Pitman be pleased and isn't this great and I wonder why the crowd are booing instead of cheering?

And then I thought myself into the position of being one of the ones who didn't start and saying to myself: "Well, Maeve, aren't you the bright little jockey. Now we only have to run nine of us and maybe I'll win in a smaller field." Because that's what the nine were told would happen.

The Jockey Club is not really the Jockey Club in anything except name; it's not a trade union for jockeys. The whole language of this sport is very suspect. They talk about my head lad, and the stable lad and I know, I know they will say that these are the terms, these are official titles with their own dignity and I am just splitting hairs and not understanding - but words have a history, and I don't think you can talk about racing, the sport of the masses, if it has such a hierarchical structure.

I remember objecting to the words of *All Things Bright and Beautiful* once because of its theory that God made everyone and gave them a position to be in: the rich man in his castle and the poor man at his gate. People said it was just a hymn, that was all. That made it 20 times worse to me, and it doesn't improve the class-ridden vocabulary of racing when anyone says it's just the jargon and everyone loves it.

The horses don't have much say; the people who ride them and who train them and those who own them all claim to love these animals and I'm sure they do. The people who handed over those staggering millions, that we are all trooping back to the bookies to collect, claim to think it's a great sport and well worth anyone's investment.

Let them rise against the Hats, the gesturers, the pointers, the people who are too steeped in tradition to put in a screen or a Tannoy or something from the 20th century that might let the horses and their riders know what's happening. We probably needed the raw hysteria and naked disappointment – making people babble inanities about Ireland being a Third World country and still being able to stop a horse race – to show what a farce it is to let old-fashioned nobs run things because they have always done so.

It's a bit hard on the few who were responsible for the particular cock-up on Saturday, but only a bit hard. Their day had to come and it was fortunate that it came so publicly, causing such rage and reaction. There's nothing left for that lot to defend. My advice is that they should come out sobbing with repentance from the inquiry and declare a new era for racing.

And maybe the backward little country here could give them some pointers about the way to go.

RETIRING TYPES

*"Maybe Des O'Malley means it when he says it is time
for young people to take the helm"*

Most people agree that women retire much more positively than men. It has nothing to do with gurgling grandchildren, coffee mornings or hours spent sitting down, doing tapestry. It has a lot to do with attitude. With the exception of Margaret Thatcher, who never lived a real life anyway and so hangs on in there pathetically like an old actor who won't leave the theatre, women see work as a phase in their lives. They don't see retirement as a yawning emptiness; they see it as a beginning.

Perhaps men of this generation are beginning to see the light and maybe Des O'Malley means it when he says it is time for young people to take the helm. It would be cheering if he *does* mean it and if he isn't looking for new helms to hold on to. It would be a positive inspiration if he decided not to root for some other job, if he were to make a statement that life was not all about work and power and achievement; cheering if he could be a man who does not define himself by his work.

Because men have been very guilty of doing that. The job *c'est moi* mentality has destroyed the lives of many men who should have had a perfectly happy 20 years or more after their retirement date but who instead believe that they have been somehow cast adrift when they still have a lot to contribute.

Of course they have a lot to contribute. It would be barking mad to get out the slippers and the secateurs and long woolly cardigan, but why does the contribution have to be only in the workplace? It's a pretty poor definition of life and hope and the time we spend between being a baby and dying, if the only meaningful bit of it is actually spent away from the home, the chosen mate and the children that resulted, away from them in a competitive scoring work situation.

I know Des O'Malley is young; he's a contemporary of my own for heaven's sake. We started out in UCD on the same day. He is, by our standards, very young indeed. He has always been vastly energetic; even at College he seemed to be involved in everything. There was nothing languid about Des. He doesn't need to have another job to define him. He is the sum of what he has done. Those who admire him, and I am one, will continue to admire him. And isn't being a TD enough? Most of us would consider that a fairly energetic way of spending dawn to dusk.

Why does there have to be huge speculation about what job he will have next, whether it's Europe or a series of directorships? Why does there have to be such analysis about his motives for going now, as if only a raving lunatic would leave a position of power unless prodded firmly by the threat of a coup?

Everyone is wailing about how the young have to emigrate and how we are educating the country's youth and have no jobs to give them. Would it not be a very positive example indeed if those who could afford to do so, and who truly believe it's time to let younger people in, actually did let them in? But for this we need a change of attitude and maybe Des is of the right generation to start that change.

Years ago, you never saw a man wheeling a pram in Ireland, you never heard of men taking paternity leave, you never believed that a man might change his job and his place of living because his wife got promoted. These things happen now all around us and we take it for granted.

Des O'Malley and I were born into a world where girls cleaned their brothers' shoes, where a man felt threatened if he could not provide for his family and he had to send his wife out to work. We have lived through decades during which the family was put under enormous strain all over Ireland because men had to work too hard and too long and were not able to enjoy their leisure. Retirement was always celebrated in a singularly inappropriate way by the presentation of a clock or a watch to mark the time that would now tick slowly past, since the meaning of life was over.

People are living longer; they don't want to go into their dotage the day they leave a job. Sensible workers are already planning schemes much more enthralling than the old-style image of making home-made wine in a potting shed and shuffling off to a local pub at lunch-time to bore everyone rigid with tales of how it used to be in the old days. Des O'Malley was always proud of what he considered to be breaking the mould in Irish politics. Let him try to do the same for Irish lifestyles as well.

No sane person would think that 54 was old, or past it, or time to settle down into some kind of reminiscent phase. But equally, no sane person would think you have to have another and better and more thrusting and eager job to be still considered an important person. If he really wants to break another mould or two, then perhaps he might consider spearheading a campaign that says you are not your job.

LADY IN WAITING

"It's very hard for a hyperactive person to be quiet"

Margaret Thatcher used to be *terrifying*. I'm talking serious fear here. On the one occasion I had to ask her a question at a press conference, I was awake all night clearing my throat for it and when I *did* get the words out, I heard a roaring in my ears and couldn't make out what she had replied.

Heads of other governments, her own ministers, the royal family, people in showbiz all reeled backwards in terror of her. I once saw a waiter fall out a window – and only saved from death by a strategically placed flower box – when she was power-walking through a dining-room looking to left and right of her with demon intent.

But now it's over. Now she should be doing something else. I've often had this fantasy that she would consult me about her next career move. That she might phone me and ask me over for a bit of girl talk. I would be offered one Scotch whisky and English Malvern water. No nasty European habits like wine.

And she would look at me with burning sincerity and want to know what would I do now, if I were her. And I'm such a big softie I'd try to give her genuine advice. I'd suggest that we look at a video of the House of Lords debate where she seems to be taking part in a sort of a pantomime.

There she was in her blue suit. Like the old days, the well-coiffed blonde hair, the mannered gestures, the total conviction that she was right. And she was talking and talking and laying down the law and booming about diminishing democracy and substituting bureaucracy. Her eyes were getting that dangerous glint as she talked of Eurospeak and drivel and fingers being burned. But, though all the lights were on, there was every sign that there was no one at home.

The House of Lords was full and, as the camera went from one face to another, they all looked embarrassed for her. Shifty almost. There they were – blasts from the past. People that you thought were dead. All the people she had raised up and then clubbed down with her handbag. Willie Whitelaw, Geoffrey Howe, Norman Tebbit. All of them shaking their locks regretfully at her.

Of course she lost the vote. And she lost a lot of friends. For the first time in 34 years she voted against her party. They won't like that.

But it's no use telling her she shouldn't have done it. It's done. It's like the times when a friend has been very drunk: you don't say she should have drunk more water in between the glasses of wine to avoid the boiled eyes and thumping head, she knows that so well. The question is: Do you give her a Bloody Mary, get her to sign the pledge or help her write the letter of apology?

What do you do for Lady Thatcher? Ask her to do the thing she's worst at. Tell her the only hope is to lie low. Even the newspapers that used to stand up for her are full of criticism these days. Increasingly they use words like manic to describe her.

She was *always* manic, but they didn't see it; it's just that it is entirely inappropriate to be manic if you're not running the shop any more.

You're meant to be gracious. Resigned, weary, sad, head-shaking, but not ranting.

It's very hard for a hyperactive person to be quiet. It's

hard for a bossyboots to let other people run things when she thinks they're running it all into the ground. Let nobody mention things like having a nice rest, or gardening, or being a proper granny, or having time for her friends to Lady Thatcher. She would look at you with mystification. She still thinks there's going to be a chance to lock horns with someone, stand like a prow, being Joan of Arcish about something, or start a good war.

No, I think if you were her friends, and had her interests at heart, you would tell her that there was something big coming up on the horizon and she should save her strength for it.

And in a way, for her, there is something coming up. Her memoirs. Called *The Downing Street Years*, as if nobody else had ever had any. *Downing Street Years* will be published on October 18th. If she had a titter of sense she would go into hiding now until the book comes out.

There will be some interest in it when it appears. To be fair, there will be considerable interest. People will want to know what she thought of others. They will read it to find out if she justifies every single thing she did or actually acknowledges the odd mistake. They will rake it for a hint of a private life or a passing involvement with her twin children anywhere along the line. They will hope that she says something cheering about Denis and not too much about Ronald Reagan.

But there are three months to go. And if she's going to be popping up burning ever more brightly, and always more meaninglessly about Europe, she's going to diminish her currency and weaken her appeal.

She doesn't need a rest. The woman only sleeps four hours a night as it is. She'd be dead in two minutes if you sent her to bed. She needs something to do to keep her from driving everyone mad.

I'd advise her to go on a three-month tour of Europe with the intention of writing a book about how much she hates everything – frogs' legs and paella and bouzouki music and Dutch cheese and Bernini statues. She'd have a great time. No one would know where she was and, when she came back to do her dinner circuit and to flog the book, they would have all forgotten how embarrassing and silly she had been this past week in the House of Lords.

In fact while she was gone, fuming up and down the Alps, muttering on Autoroutes, grumbling on Paradors, Major might have dirtied his bib more and they'd be thinking she wasn't as bad as they remembered.

It's tough, Margaret, but you did ask me round to advise you. And the best thing I can say is: Let's not hear a squeak out of you. And maybe the book on Europe will turn out to be a great success and you'll go to it with your nice closed mind and there will be no danger that you might get any nasty surprises and enjoy the place.

COLOUR HER GREY

"There has been a bit too much colour in Britain of late. They want something muted and gentle now."

If I were Norma Major, I would make a positive virtue out of being Grey. I would make Greyness the in thing, the class-act of the decade. And I would become the high priestess of it. The Greyest of all.

The country that her husband rules over is actually dying

for a bit of peaceful greyness if she only knew it. She should listen to no advisers telling her to wear bright colours and come out with bright utterances.

There has been a bit too much colour in Britain of late. They want something muted and gentle now. They want background people, and Norma could be leader of the pack.

Norma was 51 last month. Nice and quietly. Good.

There is no need for the image-makers to dredge up exciting things to feed to the press about her. Every now and then, when they think she's getting too grey, they tell us: about the oops-oops time she once said that she was "sick of her husband bringing all the official boxes home to bed with them with a clatter and a crash which was bloody selfish of him really".

Never has a phrase been so often quoted: it's as if to prove that she has spark and fire so that the great electorate won't think she is ordinary and stop voting for her husband.

But this is where they have got it so wrong. People are dying for somebody ordinary. Everyone else lives fairly dreary lives; they want leaders to be dreary too.

They are sick of flash-harry people like Norman Lamont and Fergie. They are tired of revelations about Prince Charles's friend Camilla and Fergie's father's love life. Deep down they are looking for someone gracious and non-showy, someone respectable and understated.

They have lost Queen Elizabeth. First of all her family is out of control; then she has started quibbling about the taxes she did agree to pay. No: it's Norma's big chance.

And this is how I'd do it.

I'd surround myself with the loudest and most colourful people in the land, or indeed any land. I would engineer and manipulate some kind of public event where they would all show themselves up to be deafening and vulgar and ultimately tiresome.

It might be an event in aid of a charity or a good cause and she could assemble a team of people like Fergie and Ruby Wax and Ben Elton and Lenny Henry and Jeffrey Archer and Twink – and many, many more people, good and bad, who would have one thing in common: they would all be colourful and vocal. Then she should let them loose on the media. All together.

And because they are all such troopers, people like myself, who can't abide a silence, and who rush to fill the vacuum – they will feel that things need to be said, and follow that awful principle that the Show Must Go On. And they'll be so noisy and plain tiring that the people will turn to Norma as they once turned to Eva Peron.

Don't forget Evita gave the Argentines what they didn't have, which was a bit of glamour. Norma could give the British a rest from colour and drama; she could give them a lovely safe grey haven.

If I were Norma, I would realise that I had done everything right so far. She has perfect credentials. She had a job as a domestic science teacher in various London schools. She met her husband not in a topless bar or in an eyeball-to-eyeball conflict over a boardroom table but doing constituency work, ferrying voters to and from the polls.

She has brought up her two children quietly and normally and well out of the public eye; hardly anyone knows anything about Elizabeth and James Major which is a plus for her. She has an endearing habit of saying things that turn out to be absolutely untrue.

Like saying, in 1990, that things couldn't be as bad as in 1989 when her husband had been Foreign Secretary. She thought things were going to quieten down a bit.

Then, when asked what his chances were of becoming Prime Minister she said: "That kind of thing doesn't happen to people like us."

She has laid an excellent foundation for greatness. Let her take no heed of those who want to give her public speaking lessons and assertiveness training. Instead she should be seen daily in the company of anyone whose main claim to fame is that they're a bit of a mouth. It will be such a comfort not to have to listen to anyone else with instant attitude on everything that the people will cleave to her.

The memories of being handbagged to death will only be a bad dream; the Hillary factor will not hang over them; the relief that they might have escaped being lectured by Glenys Kinnock will be extreme. Andrew Lloyd Webber could be waiting in the wings:

> *Don't cry because you're grey Normita.*
> *The truth is, that's the colour they want you.*

LILAC BUGGY

"Aer Rianta doesn't really mind if we take off or land
on an emu as long as we use their airports"

Now it is never the fault of Aer Lingus, you must understand that as you fight for breath and hold on to passing strangers for support. Because it's actually true. Aer Lingus only runs the airline. The bad guys are the British Airport Authority and Aer Rianta; their remit is all about airport management and duty-free shops and design and planning and duty-free shops and car parking and catering and duty-free shops and fire-fighting and rescue and duty-free shops.

So when Heathrow became off limits for those of us without the long, loping gait of the athlete, the stamina of the Alaskan husky and the spare canister of oxygen at the ready, a lot of us chose to use British provincial airports instead.

I picked Bristol because we have friends who live near it and it's a great excuse to go and see them and it's a dotey little airport anyway. It's like a holiday airport in Greece 30 years ago: you get off the plane and walk a short distance into a small building while your luggage chugs along beside you on a trailer. And that's it. No tunnels, no turning corners and saying "I don't believe this . . ." There's no labyrinth, no miles of terrible, menacing carpet, no series of 4,000 glossy advertisements to darken your brow. (If all these advertisers pay real money for this airport space then maybe, you fear to yourself, the journey will be twice the length next year).

So I felt a lot better, selfishly. I felt that I had found a solution to the problems posed by Heathrow's interminable terminal. And, in Dublin, there was a nice buggy that drove you down the long journey to Pier A. And all kinds of able-bodied people travelled on this buggy, so you didn't feel as if you'd thrown in the towel by getting into it.

So far, so good.

And then a few months ago, there was no buggy. Very disappointed indeed, I asked what had happened to it. They thought it might be off for the day. That was bad luck, I thought, and crawled off to make the journey down the miles of Pier A. I didn't make a federal case out of it at the time because a buggy could break down or a driver could be sick.

Two weeks later there was no buggy again. They hadn't seen one for days, people told me, so I rang Aer Rianta. It was all the work being done in the area, they said, lots of building, and it would be difficult for the buggy to navigate through all the great works that were going on to enhance Pier A. When would it eventually be enhanced, I asked? Stage One was going according to plan, I was told.

I went out to the airport last week. Stage One had gone according to plan: a gleaming duty-free shop had opened, naturally. Heavy priority. No workmen around with their bums in the air to be mown down by those travelling in buggies like they had feared before. But not a buggy to be seen.

I rang Aer Rianta again when I had recovered from the journey. It's a bit too crowded for the buggies I was told, too many people around the place. Most of them concerned about chest pains, I said.

The spokesman went away to get a ruling. The ruling came back. There were too many people around Pier A, they said, that was the problem. People coming both ways – departing and arriving. When there were only departing passengers, it meant they were all going in one direction and you could sort of skirt them in the buggy but now you'd be crashing into them and the place would be strewn with bodies. I am paraphrasing their answer.

I did suggest, mildly, that an airport authority might, in fact, expect people to be travelling in both directions, it being the nature of things. People arrive, people leave. They took this on board and said that soon, quite soon, a travelator would arrive, at enormous cost, to carry people the long, long way to Pier A. Could they hazard a guess as to how soon? The inside of a year, they hoped. And would the travelator go all the way or just a silly cosmetic little distance like at Heathrow? Nearly all the way, they hoped. But until then, would Pier A be buggyless?

Had I noticed the nice, new, little trolley things they had introduced, they wondered? To be strictly fair, I had. But I considered them a very poor substitute for our friend the buggy.

I asked why it was that, sometimes, when you came back from Bristol or Birmingham, you found yourself by a miracle in the Arrivals Hall and other times you had the Long March. It was a question of docking, they said, it all depended where the plane docked.

Now my advice to Aer Rianta is to get real. They are meant to be a service industry. They do all sorts of passenger surveys and claim that they read customer complaint cards. The profile of visitors surely includes the maturing traveller as well as those armies of lithe little back-packers who leap from every flying machine only dying to stretch their long limbs by doing a few laps around the circular terminal building. There must be many, like myself, who are not disabled enough for a wheelchair but not strong enough to fly from Pier B (which is normal) to Heathrow (which is not). And not able now to fly to Bristol or Stansted (which are normal), because it means going through Pier A in Dublin, which is getting less normal every week Next time I'll try CityJet to London City Airport to measure the normality factors.

But, you see, Aer Rianta doesn't really mind if we take off or land on an emu as long as we use their airports – and that just isn't fair. Truly, it isn't fair just to ignore the people who drag themselves along saying "It can't be much further now and it'll be over by this time tomorrow".

This is a public limited company which is meant to be working in our interests, helping us to travel to and from our own island, and helping visitors to get in and out of the place with some kind of feeling of well-being rather than submitting them to an endurance test.

I have been studying the pictures of Dermot O'Leary (Acting Chairman) and Derek Keogh (Chief Executive) in the IPA Yearbook and Diary. From the small, postage stamp-sized images they look like men with perfectly clear and open expressions. You can't see any sadism in their smiles.

But they cannot be reasonable men if they cancel passenger services such as buggy cars – especially when all they need to do is put bells on them to alert pedestrians, for heaven's sake. They can't be open and fair if they hide behind explanations about passengers travelling in both directions as if this was some sort of freaky complication – in an airport.

I advise Aer Rianta that the tumbrels could well come for them one day. Tumbrels with lovely, big, comfortable buggy wheels and seats and engines. Let them act now before it is too late.

July 16, 1994

(*Aer Rianta moved with speed to restore the buggy. Indeed, they didn't even stop to do more than give it a quick wipedown before they wheeled in onto the Pier A route, which is why it is still a pallid yellow as we go to print. However, they assure me that the minute there's a let-up in the customer traffic they are going to paint it, and you can send me a thought of gratitude as you glide up and down in the Lilac Buggy. This is the kind of response that makes giving unasked-for advice totally worthwhile.*)

The End

Also published by Poolbeg

Maeve
Binchy

The Lilac Bus

By the bestselling author of *Circle of Friends*
and *The Cooper Beech*

A collection of eight interwoven tales, brimming with
wit and laughter. The people who travel on the Lilac
Bus lead separate lives in Dublin during the week, but
are thrown together at the weekend for the journey
home to Rathdoon. Their paths begin to cross in an
unexpected and intriguing way . . .

In these stories, Maeve uses her trademark deft
touches and humour to point to the goodness and
folly of human nature.

ISBN 978-1-85371-1169

Also published by Poolbeg

Maeve Binchy

Dublin 4

By the bestselling author of *Circle of Friends*
and *The Cooper Beech*

These four stories, set in the heart of Dublin's
fashionable Southside, focus on the dilemmas facing
ordinary people.

There is – a society hostess who invites her husband's
mistress to dinner, a country girl lost in the big city, a
reformed drinkerbeset by temptations and a student
grappling with the problem of an unplanned
pregnancy.

With her intimate grasp of human feelings and her
uncanny ear for dialogue, Maeve Binchy lavishes
sympathy and affection on all her characters,
brave and foolish alike.

ISBN 978-1-85371-1022

Maeve Binchy
and
Wendy Shea

Aches & Pains

What do you want when your're miserable with
aches and pains?

a) chocolates to rot your teeth?

b) grapes with dangerous pips in them?

c)expensive flowers that will need plenty of fuss and
attention?

Or would you rather laugh out loud and cheer up?
Maeve Binchy's wonderful mixture of humour, common
sense, and anecdote will advise on everything from
Barin Your Body, Elastic Stockings and Giving Up Drink
to Cheering Things About Chest Pains.

ISBN 978-1-85371-8878